60 tips

anti-ageing

Nathalie Chassériau-Banas

HACHETTE Illustrated

contents

Note: The information and recommendations given in this book are not intended to be a substitute for medical advice. Consult your doctor before acting on any recommendations given in this book. The authors and publisher disclaim any liability, loss, injury or damage incurred as a consequence, directly or indirectly, of the use and application of the contents of this book.

21 >>> 40 TIPS

41 >>> 60 TIPS

introduction

You are 50 years old – now what happens?

It's your fiftieth birthday. Everyone knows what that means, there's no need to draw a diagram. It heralds the imminent arrival of the menopause and all that it entails. It means goodbye to youth and good looks. It's the empty nest syndrome after the children have left home and it often means a husband whose thoughts are wandering elsewhere, even if he hasn't already gone. It's about parents nearing their eighties, growing old and passing away. All in all, it's a nightmare scenario from which none of us is likely to escape unharmed.

We've been told all this time and again until we're sick and tired of it. Fortunately for us, this alarming picture is no longer true, so it's time to set the record straight. Today's fifty-year-old women are very different from those of previous generations. Many of us are still pursuing careers and we can count on powerful allies and a whole range of ways and means with which to combat the ageing process successfully. As Germaine Greer said in her book, *The Second Half of Life*, the human female is the only animal that can, after her reproductive function is over, build her own life.

Female baby boomers, aware that we are a special generation and used, since early childhood, to feel that we are fighting for a cause, are not at all disposed to tiptoe silently away and accept the bleak prospects of what our grandmothers called 'the change of life'.

The glass half empty or the glass half full

Of course, there is some truth in the gloomy picture we've been given. But every truth looks different seen from a different standpoint. Without doubt, when the ovaries stop functioning, it causes a deep physiological shock that affects all, or almost all, of the female organism. Except that, aren't we the first generation to benefit from hormone replacement therapy, which, by restoring our levels of oestrogen and progesterone, removes most of the inconveniences associated with the menopause?

Certainly, we are a long, long way from being thirty and we must accept that we have definitely reached maturity, but is that really so disastrous? Men no longer whistle at us in the street and seldom stare at us in the train but does that mean that we have ceased to exist?

Our children have left home to live their own lives or are about to leave. Is this a tragedy or the beginning of a different life? Our husband has a roving eye? That's very hard to accept but we have eyes just like him.

Let's teach ourselves to use them and to look closely at the world around us. We're bound to discover many things we didn't expect to be there. Far from being a curse, being fifty years old is an opportunity – an opportunity to change the way we look at life just at the moment when other people are changing the way they look at us; to reorganize our daily lives from top to bottom but this time, for the first time, according to our own interests and our own needs; and also the opportunity to learn about ourselves as complete and independent persons, no longer subjected to the pressing requests of children and partners.

It's up to us, up to you, to seize this opportunity or let it escape. If you seize it, you will be approaching the age of fifty in the best possible way. The glass in front of you is full to the brim with new possibilities.

If, on the other hand, you insist on seeing your glass as half empty, dwelling on what you have lost without the slightest idea of what you have to gain, your future will hardly be something to look forward to.

Giving up is out of the question

Learning to appreciate and value the passing of time does not mean being passive and resigned. Here you are, at this strange age when some women already look like grannies and others still look almost like young women. Sometimes it's the result of heredity, often of temperament, but always of effort. The aim is not to become young again but to work everyday at keeping yourself as you are now for as long as possible. Combatting ageing is not a tedious chore but it is a discipline that affects all aspects of life. You are going to have to change your habits and differently manage your spare time, your food, your beauty care, your clothes, your physical exercise and so on. The list may seem long but, rest assured, it's worth it. Ladies, on your marks, roll up your sleeves and let's go!

how to use this book

●●● FOR YOUR GUIDANCE

> A symbol at the bottom of each page will help you to identify the natural solutions available:

Herbal medicine, aromatherapy, homeopathy, Dr Bach's flower remedies – how natural medicine can help.

Simple exercises – preventing problems by strengthening your body.

Massage and manipulation – how they help to promote well-being.

Healthy eating – all you need to know about the contribution it makes.

Practical tips for your daily life – so that you can prevent instead of having to cure.

Psychology, relaxation, Zen – advice to help you be at peace with yourself and regain serenity.

> A complete programme that will solve all your health problems. Try it!

This book offers a made-to-measure programme, which will enable you to deal with your own particular problem. It is organized into four sections:

- **A questionnaire** to help you to assess the extent of your problem.
- **The first 20 tips** that will show you how to change your daily life in order to prevent problems and maintain health and fitness.
- **20 slightly more radical tips** that will develop the subject and enable you to cope when problems occur.
- **The final 20 tips** which are intended for more serious cases, when preventative measures and attempted solutions have not worked.

At the end of each section someone with the same problem as you shares his or her experiences.

You can go methodically through the book from tip 1 to 60 putting each piece of advice into practice. Alternatively, you can pick out the recommendations which appear to be best suited to your particular case, or those which fit most easily into your daily routine. Or, finally, you can choose to follow the instructions according to whether you wish to prevent stress problems occurring or cure ones that already exist.

how are you coping with the years?

Answer the following questions honestly by ticking the **yes** or **no** box, according to whether you are rarely or regularly affected by these problems.

		HEALTH
yes	no	1 Do you get tired more easily than before and take longer to recover?
yes	no	2 Have your blood pressure and/or cholesterol levels increased?
yes	no	3 Are you often depressed, stressed or unable to sleep?
yes	no	4 Has the menopause changed your life in any significant way?

		APPEARANCE
yes	no	5 Are you tending to put on weight and are your muscles tending to slacken?
yes	no	6 Are you pleased with what you see in the mirror?
yes	no	7 Do you have a big problem with wrinkles?
yes	no	8 Have you considered cosmetic surgery?

		HABITS
yes	no	9 Do you consume a lot of stimulants (tea, coffee, cigarettes, alcohol etc.)?
yes	no	10 Do you pay attention to the nutritional value of your food?
yes	no	11 Do you play sport or go to the gym regularly?
yes	no	12 Would you like more time for yourself?

If you have answered YES to questions 1, 3, 5 and 9 and NO to questions 6, 10 and 11, read Tips **1** to **20**.

If you have answered YES to questions 2, 4, 7, 8 and 12, read Tips **21** to **40** and **41** to **60**.

» **Celebrate your age:** it's great. Far from being the 'beginning of the end', your fiftieth birthday nowadays marks a new start, a new phase in your life.

»» Thanks to progress in medicine, cosmetics and nutritional science, **you can stay beautiful and fit for years to come.** Yet, the menopause is far from being a minor event: to keep what you have taken for granted up to now, you will have to make some effort.

»»» **These first 20 tips** will help you to reorganize your lifestyle and make it healthier and happier.

20
TIPS

Your silhouette changes with the years: it's a fact that can't be ignored. Learn to recognize and understand the signals your body sends you, so that you can act effectively as soon as problems appear.

listen to what your body has to say

The signs of ageing and their causes

The main signs of ageing are as follows:
• **the formation of cellulite:** water retention; unsuitable diet; lack of physical exercise (see Tips 7, 32 and 40)
• **sagging muscles, loss of skin elasticity:** reduced hormone production; lack of exercise (see Tips 11 and 19)

DID YOU KNOW?

> Unless you are physically very active, muscle mass begins to diminish and turn to fat from the age of 25. At the menopause this process becomes more obvious and also body fat changes position: the breasts and the behind tend to get smaller, whilst the waist and the stomach get larger and rounder. You will not be able to stop this from happening completely but you can control it by doing some exercises designed to work the abdominal region.

• **dry, rough skin:** reduced activity in the sebaceous glands; lack of moisturizing (see Tips 24 and 30)

• **increased waistline, appearance of a tummy:** over-production of androgens relative to oestrogens; living a sedentary life; intestinal problems (see Tips 7, 56 and 57)

• **back pain or joint pains, loss of suppleness:** osteoarthritis, beginning of decalcification (bone loss leading to osteoporosis); muscular tension (see Tips 9 and 14)

• **sagging and shrinking breasts:** lack of oestrogen directly caused by the menopause; inevitable consequence of the law of gravity (see Tips 39 and 50).

Make sure you don't get a tummy

That's your first objective. Change your eating habits so you don't suffer from a distended stomach. Take more time over your meals, chew them more, reduce the amount of raw vegetables, garlic and onions you eat (to avoid wind and bloating). Avoid constipation by walking more, drinking more water and adding fibre to your breakfast cereals. Make sure you stand up straight and hold in your tummy.

> Remember this when choosing a new sport or new gym exercises as a part of your daily routine.

KEY FACTS

* Once a week look at yourself naked in the mirror.

* A large stomach and lack of agility will age you more far than wrinkles.

* To avoid getting a tummy, do some abdominal exercises every day.

You can do nothing to prevent long-sightedness: after the age of 45 glasses become a fact of life. This can be a shock for those women who have never worn them before. All the more reason to invest in attractive glasses that enhance the way you want to look.

make your glasses an attractive accessory

Now and again or all the time?

If bifocals and half-moon glasses are out of the question, you are left with two options: multifocals (varifocals), which allow you to see things at various distances, and 'reading' glasses, which only correct your close vision. The first, although considerably more expensive, can be worn all day without giving away the fact that you are long-sighted. However, you may find it hard to do

●●● DID YOU KNOW?

> You will begin to show signs of long-sightedness between the ages of 40 and 45. It is caused by a problem of accommodation due to the ageing of the crystalline lens, which loses its elasticity in the course of time.

> When looking at close objects, rays of light no longer converge correctly on the retina and the image is blurred. The capacity of accommodation gradually gets worse until the age of 60 and then remains about the same.

without them, even when you are wearing an evening dress or playing sport. As for the second type, you will have to get used to constantly taking them on and off and frequently looking for them. The answer to this is to buy some cords of different colours that match your different outfits and wear your glasses around your neck without giving it a second thought. Accepting your long-sightednesss is the first step towards accepting your age.

Frames really matter

It's worth taking time over the choice of frames, because glasses that don't suit your face will put ten years on you. Their shape and colour definitely must not clash with your style and personality. When you're trying them on, look at yourself in a compact mirror and direct it towards a larger one. This will give you a better idea of how others will see you.

Ask a friend to go with you to the optician's, as the advice of a third person is always valuable. If your budget allows it, invest in three or four different frames, so that you can match them with your different clothes.

> At the present time, long-sightedness cannot be prevented or delayed. You will have to wait some years before an operation is available. In the meantime there are always contact lenses, which are improving all the time (see Tip 52).

*

KEY FACTS

* Buy hard cases for your glasses – they will offer better protection. Choose a brightly-coloured case – it will be much easier to find in your handbag.

* Hang spare pairs of glasses by a cord in all 'strategic' places, such as the bathroom and the kitchen.

Reduced production of hormones from the ovary, sometimes known as the 'serenity hormone', can cause a tension you won't have experienced before. Learn how to to relax, anytime and anywhere.

03 give stress the boot

Breathe from the diaphragm

The first thing to do in order to relax is to learn how to breathe correctly. To do this, you must use the diaphragm, the dome-shaped muscle situated at the base of the thorax (chest). Stand with your shoulders relaxed, hands on hips, and breathe in deeply. Let your stomach swell like a balloon. Hold your breath for around 2 or 3 seconds, then breathe out slowly. Repeat at least a dozen times.

1

2

3

Some yoga exercises to help keep you calm

Do each of these exercises at least ten times.

• Stand with hands together, fingers linked. Turn your palms upwards and lift your arms above your head, stretching them right up. Hold the position for 10 to 15 seconds. Repeat the exercise with the palms turned downwards.

• Kneel, breathe in deeply from the diaphragm and lift your arms above your head, fingers linked, palms facing upwards. Stretch your arms and spine as far as you can. Breathe out.

• Sit with one leg bent over the other, back straight, hands held together over your head and breathe in slowly from the diaphragm. Hold your breath for 2 to 3 seconds and then breathe out slowly. Change legs and repeat.

• Sit with your left leg stretched out in front of you, your right leg bent and your left arm behind your back. Try to touch the toes of your left foot with your right hand. Hold the position for 20 seconds. Swap arms and legs and repeat.

DID YOU KNOW?

> You can use several techniques to get rid of stress.

> Kundalini yoga uses physical, mental and spiritual energy to contribute to the development of the body.

> Ayurvedic massage originated in India. It is a comprehensive form of massage, which helps energies to circulate and relaxes tension.

> Fascial massage is a gentle, deep method that detects zones of tension and eliminates them by working on precise points.

> Shiatsu massage is a method that is carried out through the clothes and involves pressing the acupuncture meridians with the fingers.

KEY FACTS

* In moderate doses stress helps you to stay young, because it causes the secretion of adrenaline, which preserves the reflexes. It is excessive stress that must be avoided.

* Twice a day do some deep breathing from the diaphragm.

04 reconsider the way you dress

Dressing fashionably doesn't mean trying to look like someone in their twenties. Your body and your mind are changing. The time has come to adapt your style to suit the new you.

Avoid at all costs: cropped tops which reveal your navel; miniskirts; body piercings; hair that is overly long; garishly dyed hair (beware of 'menopause red'!); anything your mother-in-law wears.

Choose only occasionally and with care: cheap jewellery; sequins; fabrics with leopard or python prints; stiletto heels; trainers and other trendy footwear loved by teenagers; dark colours close to your face, because they make you look unwell; everything your daughter loves.

Bear in mind your new shape: has your waist thickened a bit? No more thin, tight belts! Instead choose wide ones, worn a little loose just above the hips. Is your tummy a little more round? Hide it with long jackets or blouses. Have your breasts become saggy? Dare to wear an uplift bra (see Tip 39).

DID YOU KNOW?

> Never buy your clothes when you're in a hurry. Always give yourself plenty of time to have a good look around.

> Find out which colours make you look good by trying on clothes in daylight. Always buy good quality accessories.

KEY FACTS

* Stay slim and you'll be able to wear whatever you like.

* Pretend you are a fashion editor. Get all your clothes out of your wardrobe and invent new combinations.

05 dance and stay young

'A single day without dancing is a day wasted,' said Nietzsche. Even if you haven't danced for decades, there's nothing to stop you from starting again, with or without your partner.

Begin by dancing at home. Put on some leggings, a leotard and some ballet shoes. Choose the rhythms you like best. It doesn't matter if it's rock, salsa or techno as long as you're dancing. Twenty minutes of dancing a day will do wonders for your mood, improve your breathing and blood circulation, burn off calories and help you feel sexier. Dancing is a pleasure and excellent exercise. Don't do without it!

Enrol at a dance school! It's time to fulfil one of your old dreams and learn to dance (well) as a couple. If your partner wants to, take him along. If not, go with a friend (male or female) and become an expert in the Argentinian tango (very fashionable these days), the waltz or the jive. You will discover that you can dance whatever your age, you will make friends and find new self-confidence.

DID YOU KNOW?

There are many types of dance to choose from, including:

> Argentinian tango

> Traditional dance

> Salsa

> Rock and roll

KEY FACTS

* Dancing will make you feel euphoric and sexy. It will encourage you to take care over your appearance and feel good about yourself.

* Enjoy again the pleasure of going out dancing with your friends.

* Instead of having dinner parties, go dancing!

When you reach fifty or so, you tend to sleep less and wake up more often. To avoid spending precious time staring anxiously at the ceiling, you're going to need to change your habits and possibly your bedtime.

get a good night's sleep

Seven tips for a good night's sleep

• Have a light meal at least two and a half hours before going to bed. Digesting a late meal is likely to disturb your sleep.
• Open your bedroom window. The air needs to circulate even in winter.
• Take a bath before going to bed. Pour in some relaxing bath oils.
• Invest in a good quality bed. Your mattress must be firm but with enough 'give'

DID YOU KNOW?

> Some people swear by the hormone melatonin (see Tip 44). Produced by the pineal gland, this substance regulates your body clock and helps you regain your usual sleep pattern after changes of time zones. Melatonin can calm you and reduce bodily tension, making you feel peaceful and sleepy. However, it is not a licensed indication in the UK and may be hard to obtain.

to accommodate the natural curve of your spine.

• Scatter a few drops of lavender essential oil on your pillow. It will help you to go to sleep.

• If daylight penetrates into your bedroom, get used to wearing a mask like those you are given on aeroplanes.

• If your partner snores, change bedrooms or buy some earplugs.

The teachings of Feng Shui

The Chinese, masters of the art of furnishing their home according to the principle of harmony between the yin and the yang, have converted the West to Feng Shui. Here are some of its teachings:

Don't place your bed between two doors. The energy, which circulates from one to the other, is likely to, metaphorically, cut you in two. Don't put a folding screen around the bed. This could prevent good energy from reaching you. Don't put the bed under a window. Don't put a ceiling light or wall lights above the bed, because electrical circuits affect your health while you are sleeping. Take all books out of your bedroom, because this room is reserved for love and rest.

> The good old folk remedies still work: avoid all drinks containing caffeine after four o'clock in the afternoon and try to drink a cup of warm milk with honey before going off to bed.

KEY FACTS

* Avoid everything that causes worry or excitement in the hour before going to bed. No television in the bedroom, no reading the newspaper, no work or payment of bills.

* If you wake up before everyone else, get up and take advantage of this moment of freedom. That evening go to bed earlier.

think thin

As you get older, your metabolism starts to slow down: your body takes longer to burn up calories and so you put on weight. Now's the time to discover how to eat both less and more healthily.

No more diets

Slimming diets are bound to fail, because, as soon as you stop dieting, you quickly put back all the weight you have lost. A better method is to reduce the size of the portions and to be more selective about what you eat. To eat less whilst still enjoying your food, take the advice of a psychologist: adopt the habit of leaving at least a quarter of your meal on the plate. This way you'll learn to eat less as well as realising there's nothing wrong with leaving some of the food you've been served.

DID YOU KNOW?

> Keeping your weight down is not all that matters. You must also stop cellulite from forming on the lower half of your body. The main contributory factors are cooked meats, fried fish, animal fats, sauces, salt (it encourages water retention), wine and other forms of alcohol, physical inactivity, stress and overwork as well as tight clothes that bulge and impede the circulation.

Avoid too much fat

Fat contains 9 calories per gram, compared with only 4 calories per gram in proteins and carbohydrates. Make sure you remove the fat from ham; choose white meats; cook with olive oil (it's the only one that remains stable at high temperatures); soak up excess any fat from food with a paper towel; beware of rich sauces. Grill, steam or stir fry rather than fry your food.

Don't skip meals

You must eat a decent breakfast. Eat a snack if you can't hold out until lunchtime: a banana between 10 and 11 o'clock is ideal. Choose a mixed salad for lunch and keep the fruit for when you feel a bit peckish at about 4 o'clock. Don't eat dessert at dinner. Put it to one side and if you still feel hungry later in the evening, you can eat it then.

> To help prevent cellulite, eat a healthier diet and take exercise (jogging, walking, cycling or swimming) that particularly involves the lower half of the body.

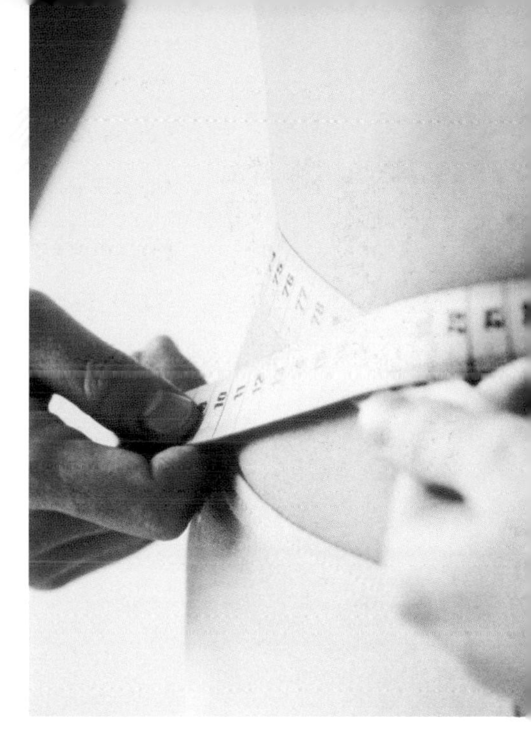

KEY FACTS

* Avoid foods containing refined carbohydrates, such as sweets and biscuits.
* Skip animal fats but not proteins, or you will lose muscles and vitality.
* To make your dishes more tasty, use spices and fine herbs in your cooking.

Free radicals cause our body cells to age but antioxidants (vitamins and trace elements) put up fierce resistance. Antioxidants are present in large quantities in fresh fruit and vegetables. So eat plenty of them!

fill up on fruit and vegetables

Antioxidants are important

A balanced diet ought to provide all the nutriments the body needs. However, modern methods of food preparation can destroy some of these precious substances. Our capacity to assimilate nutriments also declines as we get older. It is often necessary, therefore, to take some food supplements but only in

DID YOU KNOW?

> To ensure you eat good quality fruit and vegetables, go shopping several times a week, and always choose produce that is in season.

> Maximum variety: according to a fashionable theory, you ought to consume at least three different vegetables and two different fruits per day, some in juice form. So you'd better buy a juice extractor!

consultation with your doctor (see Tip 38). To improve your daily diet, eat a variety of fresh fruit and vegetables every day.

Steam your vegetables

Cooking in boiling water destroys most of the antioxidants found in fruit and vegetables. So steam them and be sure not to overcook them. Some fruit and vegetables can be cooked in the microwave with good results, in particular courgettes (zucchini), chicory, apples and pears.

> **If you can afford it, buy organic fruit and vegetables as they are usually richer in nutriments. To make your vegetable menus more varied and interesting, find out more about vegetarian cooking.**

KEY FACTS

* By eating three fruits and two vegetables per day, you may reduce by 80% the risk of developing a cancer.

* To spice up your mixed salads, try adding low-fat yoghurt mixed with lemon juice and chopped fine herbs.

Stay younger by keeping agile and supple. Follow the example of cats and stretch whenever you can. It's the best way of putting back your vertebrae, squeezed together by a sedentary lifestyle, into their correct position.

exercise your joints

Enjoy the benefits of stretching

You need to stretch to resist the way the bones of the skeleton sink. It is one of the most effective methods of preventing osteoarthritis and maintaining natural, long-lasting suppleness. Ideally, do 2 to 3 minutes of stretching four times a day.

Three exercises to do anywhere

① Keeping your legs apart, breathe in and place your forearms on a surface level with your pelvis. Breathe out, lift your hands, spread your fingers and turn your feet outwards. Move your pelvis from right to left.

② Sit up straight on a stool and hold your hands together behind your back with the palms facing downwards. Look straight ahead of you and lift your hands as high as possible, keeping the bottom of your back straight.

③ Sit up straight with outstretched arms, breathe in and put your hands together in front of you. Breathe out, lifting your hands in the air as you do so. Imagine there is a string drawing your head towards the ceiling.

●●● DID YOU KNOW?

> Each day your vertebrae sink under your weight. The pressure is greatest when you are in the sitting position. It decreases when you are standing up, and is even lower still when you are lying down.

> Do some stretching exercises before you go to bed. Your spinal column will go back into place and get the maximum benefit from its night's rest.

> Physical exercise of any sort is the best thing for your joints, because the movement makes your cartilages vibrate. These vibrations release electrolytes, such as sodium and potassium. The electrical current resulting from this release, encourages the reproduction of cartilages, a process that tends to slow down with the menopause.

KEY FACTS

* Start your exercises gently. You risk pulling a muscle if you stretch too far before you've warmed up.

* Take time out twice a day to do some stretching exercises behind your desk.

You've known for a long time that tobacco is a health hazard. What you may be less aware of is that it speeds up all the ageing processes, with disastrous consequences for your appearance.

stop smoking!

Tobacco spoils your beauty

Smoking narrows the blood vessels and reduces the amount of oxygen reaching the cells. The effect on your skin is immediately obvious: it becomes duller and yellower because the tiny blood vessels that supply it are deprived of some of their haemoglobin, the red blood pigment. In addition, cigarettes are a cause of wrinkles and contribute to the slackening of body tissue. Finally, they turn your teeth yellow and help to make your gums recede.

How to stop smoking

In 50% of cases success is entirely a matter of willpower on the part of the smoker. However, you could find it helpful to try nicotine substitutes like patches and gum. If you prefer natural methods, you might try:

- **acupuncture:** the aim of which is to make you feel disgusted with tobacco. Acupuncture has the added advantage of helping to reduce nervousness as well as avoiding insomnia;
- **homeopathy:** which gradually breaks the habit by means of minute doses of tobacco extracts;
- **auricular therapy:** which involves keeping a thread of nylon in the centre of the outer ear for three weeks. It is based on the principle that, by irritating the part of the ear that corresponds to the body's need to smoke, the craving will be eliminated.

If none of these methods work, you might consider specialized psychotherapy or hypnosis.

DID YOU KNOW?

> Cigarettes do not only contain nicotine and tar. When you light up, you also get a mouthful of benzopyrene and metals like lead, cadmium, mercury and arsenic, which the body retains in its vital organs. Cigarettes also produce an enormous amount of free radicals – the enemies of youthfulness: just one puff releases millions and millions of them!

> Also remember that cigarettes are directly responsible for emphysema and 80% of lung tumours. They are also known to harden the arteries and help to cause high blood pressure and cardiovascular diseases. If all that wasn't enough, they also accelerate decalcification and destroy antioxidants.

KEY FACTS

* A very reliable study has shown that smoking one cigarette reduces your life by 11 minutes.

* It is known that consuming tobacco and alcohol together increases the risk of throat cancer 43 times and the risk of cancer of the nasal passages 135 times.

Our figure sags because of reduction of muscle mass but also because of lack of exercise and our natural tendency to hunch forward, especially when sitting down. These last two aspects need urgent attention.

move that body!

Work those muscles

Get up earlier and go to work on foot. If it's too far, do half the journey on public transport and the other half on foot. Park some distance from home and walk the rest of the way. Make a habit of climbing the stairs. Use the lunch break for exercise two or three times a week. Go to the gym, swim or jog.

●●● DID YOU KNOW?

> As you get older, the amount of collagen in your muscles dwindles. The first signs are usually seen on the inside of the arms and thighs. Swimming is a very useful way of combatting this process.

> Walking is good for you for many reasons. Because it improves your breathing, it helps your cells to absorb more oxygen and so preserves muscle tone.

Do whatever is most practical and pleasant. If you live in a town where pollution is not a problem, consider travelling around by bike. Tighten your buttock muscles several times a day and your abdominals all the time. This will help to strengthen them.

Walking is the best medicine

Stride forward, head high, breathing regularly. To keep your hands free and back straight, use a backpack. Take a tip from the women of New York – carry your town shoes in your bag and walk to work in your trainers (sneakers). To get even fitter, wear weighted bands around your ankles and/or wrists (on sale in sports shops).

> It also prevents cellulite from forming. Ideally, walk for 40 minutes every day: a good habit that you will be able to continue until a ripe old age.

Stand up straight!

Shoulders hunched, back bent forward, stomach slack: this, unfortunately, is the way most people usually sit at their desks. When you're at work, try as often as you can to keep your back straight and your stomach in. This will strengthen your back and abdominal muscles and in turn make you look younger and feel more energetic.

KEY FACTS

* Walking non-stop for an hour at average speed will burn off 230 calories.

* Invest in good shoes – neither too heavy nor too light. The sole should be supple but thick enough to deaden the impact as your foot hits the ground.

drink a little wine and plenty of water

Good quality wine, especially if it's red, has an excellent effect on your mood and on your health, provided you limit yourself to two glasses a day and drink plenty of water the rest of the time.

The benefits of wine: two glasses of red wine will help to keep you healthy and young thanks to its tannins, which contain polyphenol, a powerful antioxidant. Choose good vintages and avoid cheap wines, which contain a lot of chemicals. It has been proved that moderate consumption of red wine increases life expectancy: more non-wine drinkers than wine-drinkers suffer from cancer and heart problems.

The dangers of wine: four or more glasses of wine per day will greatly accelerate ageing. You run a higher risk of getting cancer of the digestive tract and the liver, and you damage your brain cells. The brain of a 30-year-old alcoholic resembles that of a 50-year-old man. In addition, drinking too much wine is very likely to make you look uglier by bloating your face and bursting the little blood vessels that supply your skin.

DID YOU KNOW?

> If you've drunk an excessive amount of alcohol one evening, drink three times the same amount of water and avoid alcohol at the next few meals. In normal circumstances, drink at least 1.5 litres (two and a half pints) of liquid per day.

KEY FACTS

* Instead of coffee and ordinary tea, drink herbal teas.

* Drink water but be reasonable about it or you are liable to overwork your kidneys.

13 watch out for superfluous hair

Your body hair is also affected by the hormonal changes. Less oestrogen means more facial hair, whilst the hair on your body tends to disappear.

Spot a hair and remove it! You'll need: a magnifying mirror on your bathroom wall (if possible with a lamp nearby), a small magnifying mirror to keep in your handbag and two pairs of good quality tweezers, one for the bathroom, one for your bag. Wage war daily against new ugly black hairs, especially those over the upper lip and on the chin. Don't let anyone else use your tweezers. Your spotty adolescent son squeezing his spots may give you a skin infection.

What about downy hair? If you have blond or chestnut brown hair and a pale complexion, you might notice more blond down on your face and forearms as you get older. You can remove it with wax but it will grow back more thickly and be more noticeable. It is best just to remove the longest down on the sides of your face with tweezers and leave the rest alone.

●●● DID YOU KNOW?

> If you want a permanent solution, you can opt for electrolysis, which consists of destroying the follicle of each hair with a sterilized needle, or laser hair removal.

> These two long and expensive methods are only advisable if a very large amount of unwanted hair is involved.

KEY FACTS

* HRT (Hormonal Replacement Therapy) can slow down the growth of facial hair and the loss of pubic hair.

* Never use a razor, cream or foam and especially not on the face. They can accelerate hair growth.

Osteoporosis is called the 'silent thief', because it has no symptoms. It is often hereditary and is caused by a lack of minerals in the bones, which affects all women from the age of fifty onwards. It is, however, possible to prevent it.

don't take your bones for granted

An update on calcium

The mineral, calcium, is a major component of bones, giving them their solidity. The reduction of oestrogens, caused by the menopause, means that calcium tends to move from the bones to other parts of the body where it is harmful (cartilages, tendons, urinary tract, crystalline lens). It is, therefore, necessary to control your intake of calcium but most

DID YOU KNOW?

> Mineral loss in the bones affects all women over fifty but to different degrees. Osteoporosis, which is caused by mineral loss, makes bones brittle and therefore more vulnerable to fractures, particularly fractures of the neck of the thighbone, the vertebrae and the wrist.

> The main risk factor is heredity but there are others, such as smoking, too little calcium in the diet, a sedentary lifestyle or a lack of oestrogens, such as may be due to and an early menopause. Women with a history of absent periods caused by anorexia

of all, to help direct it towards your bones. To do that you need other substances: first and foremost, vitamin D. You can create this yourself by sunbathing (taking the necessary precautions). You can also absorb it from within by eating oily fish and eggs. In addition, you need zinc, vitamin C, vitamin B6, vitamin K and finally silicon. Eat five or six portions of fruit and vegetables per day to help meet these needs. The amount of vitamin D you require increases with age and after the menopause the recommended daily intake of vitamin D is 400-800 units with calcium. Do not exceed this level.

Help your bones by making your muscles strong

Physical exercise is vital for healthy bones. The more muscle you have, the better your bones will be supported. Muscles contribute in another way: by bringing more blood to the bones and thus helping bone cells to reproduce. If you take part in a physical activity twice a week for a year, your bone density will increase by 1% instead of decreasing by 2.5%, as is the case with most menopausal women who take no exercise. The most suitable activities are walking, cycling, stretching, dancing, jogging and gymnastics.

or an athletic lifestyle may not have laid down as much bone as others by the menopause and may be at risk of osteoporosis.

> You can have the density of your bones measured. The examination is both painless and quick.

KEY FACTS

* HRT (Hormone Replacement Therapy) can treat flushes and sweats and help prevent osteoporosis.

* To prevent a lack of calcium in your body, eat dairy foods, almonds (7 per day), bean sprouts, tofu and millet.

The menopause affects the body on different levels, having psychological as well as physical effects. So, it is the ideal time to discover holistic therapies which treat the whole individual.

think holistic

The holistic approach

The term 'holistic' comes from a Greek word meaning 'whole'. It is used to describe therapies that consider the individual as a being equipped with its own system of regulating illness. Unlike traditional western medicine, which is usually only concerned with eliminating a symptom by treating a part of the body, holistic therapies seek to restore

DID YOU KNOW?

> Every pain, every feeling of tension expends energy. The osteopath sets out to free this energy, so that it can benefit the whole being.

> The therapy is in two parts: a diagnosis of the patient's whole situation and the problems to be treated; the different types of therapeutic manipulation that cure these problems.

balance within the whole individual. Their purpose, therefore, is to help the body adapt to and compensate for attacks upon it by diseases etc. Homeopathy is the most well known of these therapies but there are others, such as acupuncture, traditional Chinese medicine, naturopathy, herbal medicine and osteopathy.

Osteopathy, a rapidly developing discipline

The principal tools of the osteopath are his or her hands. They are trained to diagnose bodily imbalances and tensions, and restore the whole being to health. There are two forms of manipulation: one that works on the skeleton, the internal and other organs, the circulatory system and the neurological system; the other that seeks to re-establish a good flow of energy around the body.

> After a session patients almost instantly feel a sensation of general contentment and renewal of energy. Osteopathy can be very beneficial during the menopause, as it, among other therapies, regulates hormones secreted in the nerve cells.

KEY FACTS

* The osteopath is not merely concerned with curing back pains but also with restoring the whole balance of structure and energy within the individual.

* In some cases a single session is enough but a series of monthly sessions can have a profound effect on your general well-being.

16 stay friends with the sun

You need the sun: it gives you a good colour, improves your mood and does even more for your bones. But make sure you don't overdo the sunbathing, because this friend can become dangerous and make your skin look irreparably old.

DID YOU KNOW?

> Ultra-violet rays destroy collagen and elastin fibres, which give the skin its elasticity, causing the face to wrinkle and the tissues to wither.

> The sun also stimulates the production of free radicals, the unstable oxygen molecules that cause ageing by stealing electrons from the body's cells and, in the process, damaging the cells. Free radicals, some of which cause cancer, encourage the formation of brown spots (liver spots) on the parts of

Sunbathe sensibly

Getting a tan is an art. It's a matter of enabling your body to produce melanin (the natural pigment which protects your skin by colouring it) in the best possible circumstances. Gradually increase the time you spend sunbathing but always avoid the hours when the sun is at its highest (the hours immediately before and after midday), because that is when its rays strike you vertically and penetrate much more deeply. Always put on suncream, changing the protection factor according to how tanned you are. Choose high factors to begin with and lower ones as the melanin takes over.

Try self-tanning

A week before leaving for your holiday in the sun, prepare your skin at a beauty salon. Treat yourself to a programme of exfoliation (removal of dead skin), light touch massage (effleurage), massage with oils that make your skin glossy and an application of self-tanning cream. These products which have a base of fruit acids (AHA/Alpha Hydroxy Acids) and erythrulose or vegetable extracts should be used in addition to sunscreens to boost your tanning. You can also help your skin 'from the inside' by taking sun capsules with a base of carotene and selenium. However, consult your doctor before taking any capsules: high doses of carotene can poison the liver.

the body most exposed to sunlight: hands, face, neck and shoulders. As if that isn't enough, they also weaken your hair by damaging its keratin. To protect yourself, use special products and recovery treatments that should preferably be applied in the evenings (oils, masks, balms and capillary foams).

KEY FACTS

* Don't expose naked breasts to the sun or you may increase the risk of developing a cancer.
* At all times protect your hands, face, neck and shoulders with sunblock.
* When on holiday, always apply an after-sun or a particularly nourishing body cream every evening.

Lack of energy is not always the result of the menopause. You can feel exhausted at any age. However, around the age of fifty, some women feel shattered most of the time. You can't just ignore this!

shattered? – do something about it!

Get your doctor's opinion

Your lack of energy and tiredness might be caused by a number of things, including a lack of vitamins or trace elements. For example, lack of potassium creates a sensation of muscle fatigue. Speak to your doctor, who will probably prescribe a blood test. Speak to your doctor, who will probably prescribe a blood test to check for conditions such as diabetes, thyroid problems or anaemia.

●●● DID YOU KNOW?

> During the menopause many women are affected by recurrent bouts of exhaustion. These women are usually experiencing a difficult menopause and are finding it hard to come to terms with. The cause of the exhaustion could, to a certain extent, be psychosomatic or due to a condition such as anaemia.

> But it is also due to the loss of hormones. The origin of the problem urgently needs to be discovered in order for it to be treated as effectively as possible.

Seven tips for overcoming tiredness

If you suddenly feel 'all in', choose the 'therapy' most suited to your situation.

• Go out and walk for 20 minutes at a good pace or go for a bicycle ride.

• Even if you would love a coffee, drink a large glass of water. Always have a bottle of mineral water to hand.

• Open the windows in the room to freshen up the air, close them again, then spray the room with an invigorating scent from an aromatherapy spray (jasmine oil, peppermint or eucalyptus).

• Hop on the spot 50 to 60 times. Oxygen will flow into your bloodstream and give you a boost.

• Go out into the light. If there's no sunshine, turn on all the lights indoors.

• Breathe at least 12 times from the diaphragm (see Tip 3).

• Laugh as much as possible. Nothing gives you more energy!

> Your GP will be able to deal with possible shortages of nutriments or physical illness and might prescribe HRT if the problem is due to lack of oestrogen. On the other hand, if the causes of exhaustion are psychological, get specialist help without delay (see Tip 59).

KEY FACTS

* Tiredness is often due to a lack of oxygen in the bloodstream. To rectify this, breathe, move, go outside.

* Consider yoga. If you do it regularly, it can cause a lasting increase in your energy level.

18 smile, it suits you!

A genuine and spontaneous smile is an immense asset. It reflects your responsiveness to others and your self-confidence. However, the most dazzling of smiles will lose much of its charm if your teeth and breath aren't up to standard.

Keeping your teeth white

As you get older, your tooth enamel becomes porous and absorbs coloured substances more easily. Cigarettes, tea and coffee are the main reasons why teeth go yellow. To stop this from becoming permanent, don't stint on the amount of time spent brushing (at least 2 minutes, 2 or 3 times a day). Electric toothbrushes are much more efficient,

DID YOU KNOW?

> Adverts only show people who are smiling or laughing loudly but, in reality, most faces are closed and sullen. This is a pity, because an open, smiling face is a gift not only to others but to ourselves: by lifting up the corners of the mouth, which naturally tend to curve downwards, smiling not only stimulates the facial muscles but prevents the lower part of the face from sagging as quickly as it might have done otherwise. Once past fifty, our facial appearance depends largely upon our expressions.

particularly at reaching the inner surface of your teeth. Scatter bicarbonate of soda (available in pharmacies) on your toothpaste. Twice a year have the tartar removed from your teeth.

Check your breath

Bad breath is very unpleasant for those who have to smell it. If you have doubts about the freshness of your breath, don't hesitate to ask your friends and family. Many people are unaware of their problem and so inflict unknowingly it on those around them, who feel too awkward to mention it. The causes of bad breath could be stress, bad digestion (particularly constipation) or an unbalanced diet. Talk to your doctor about it. It could also be due to bits of food stuck between the teeth, something that gets worse as you get older because your gums recede. After meals always clean your teeth with dental floss, electric toothbrush heads when at the office or a dental water jet when at home.

> To prevent your features from sagging, smile as often as possible and try this exercise several times a day: laugh out loud and then, exaggerating your facial muscles, pronounce 'X' and 'U' emphatically.

KEY FACTS

* Laugh, it may be good for your health! You release immunoglobulin A, which stimulates your immune system and protects you from infections.

* To have good breath, do as the Orientals do: scrape your tongue with a steel spatula to remove bacteria.

don't feel inferior to men

You use up a tremendous amount of energy in order to stay young, beautiful, active and dynamic. To please yourselves – yes – but above all to continue to please 'them'. When all this effort starts to get you down, take a little look at them: they're getting older too!

They age more quickly than you

Man seeks his pleasure, woman seeks to please. This is undeniable and explains many of the differences in behaviour between the sexes. Magazines, television, family, the whole of society 'compel' a woman to be beautiful and desirable and, if she isn't, she ceases to be considered a woman. The pressure is immense and we submit to it meekly, sometimes

DID YOU KNOW?

> The menopause is a biological revolution. When the ovaries stop functioning, it means not only the end of fertility but also a severe lack of sexual hormones. The man undergoes nothing like this hormonal revolution and can remain fertile all his life.

> However, research has shown that the level of 'available' testosterone in about 30 to 40% of men reduces significantly from middle age onwards.

blindly. As for a man, he doesn't worry too much about his appearance. One look at the prematurely bald heads, the paunches and the hardly seductive love handles ought to be enough to lift your spirits when you're feeling blue...and to be proud that you're fifty and looking after yourself so much better.

They have their problems too

The male menopause can arrive surreptitiously, settle in and develop all without the man knowing. The most obvious symptom – and the only one that really seems to bother men – is decline in sexual performance. This is even more difficult for men to go through, because they know little or nothing about their own physiology and are a million miles away from thinking that their erection difficulties might be due to hormonal causes. This new situation is often accompanied by a loss of energy and lack of motivation, sometimes depression. A dose of hormones would establish if the problem actually was a lack of testosterone (less than 2,000 pg/ml), in which case it would be totally feasible to consider replacement therapy, along the same lines as women.

> So we can talk about an andropause or male menopause, but the term remains vague and has none of the same implications as the menopause itself. The decline in sperm production (hypogonadism) varies greatly from individual to individual and can be spread over 20 years (between 45 and 65).

KEY FACTS

* It's tricky for a couple approaching the fifty-year mark and facing up to the fact that they are both getting old, but they must do all they can to keep communicating.

* If your partner 'is no longer the man he was', don't, above all, make a drama of it. Encourage him to see a doctor and not to give up trying.

20 rediscover your powers of seductiion

If you accept your age and value your experience of life as it deserves, you will discover that your seductive powers, far from having disappeared, can in fact increase.

The importance of a fit, trim body: with women as with men, the decline of sexual desire is far from having merely hormonal causes. The awareness of having put on weight and of having a less firm body can lead some women to avoid sex, because they feel less desirable. Their partner's appearance can be another factor, as well as monotony and the general wear and tear of life.

Reinvent your sex life: to be able to please others, you must first be pleased with yourself! Regaining a good figure and muscle tone will make you feel so much better and more confident in yourself. Rediscover your old fantasies or think up some new ones, so that you feel erotic again. You can reinvent your sex life at fifty but you must be able to talk about it with your partner or it just won't work!

DID YOU KNOW?

> During the menopause the cells in the ovaries that produce oestrogen and progesterone gradually waste away.

> The adrenal glands continue to produce some oestrogen and testosterone. This may help to maintain an interest in sex.

KEY FACTS

* Keep your body in 'good erotic order' with massages, perfumed creams and lingerie.
* Stay fit and trim.
* Trust in your new powers of seduction, which are no longer merely physical.

case study

50 years old... and all my life ahead of me!

'The year leading up to my fiftieth birthday wasn't a very good one. I was worried about this landmark, worried about becoming a fifty-year-old, which to my mind meant 'ugly old woman'. However, a couple of months before the fateful day the idea of organizing a big party suddenly came to me. I had some invitation cards printed on which I depicted myself as a friendly witch, jauntily perched on a broomstick in the middle of a starry sky. What did it say on them? 'Fifty years old, a reason to celebrate!' Everyone came and it was a great party. That evening I decided I would never hide my age and that, in fact, I had good reason to be proud of it. I also set up a fitness programme: 40 minutes jogging every morning, swimming two evenings a week and cycling every weekend in the countryside. That has really improved my figure and I don't have to follow any particular slimming diet'.

›› **Count yourself lucky.** Just as you're beginning to really feel the need for it, the beauty care industry is coming to your aid and concentrating its efforts on your beauty problems.

›››› Is your face starting to show signs of fatigue? You are among the first fortunate consumers to have products available that are specially prepared for 'mature' skins. Are grey hairs beginning to seriously worry you? You can make them disappear at home in less than an hour with a range of hair dyes that are improving all the time.

›››››› Today's fifty-year-olds are getting more and more attention from the cosmetics industry and the media. **It would be a sin not to take advantage of it!**

40
TIPS

become a beauty care expert

Only a few years ago, women over 45 had nothing more than unbranded anti-wrinkle products to help them. Nowadays they have their own niche in the cosmetics market. The result is better and better products specially designed to meet the extra needs of their skin.

The active substances in the new beauty care products

- **Fruit acids and AHAs (Alpha Hydroxy Acids):** their exfoliating effect freshens up the face but they can also accelerate the natural thinning of the skin. Use with care.
- **Antioxidants (in particular vitamins E and C and beta-carotene):** they are extracted from certain plants and neutralize free radicals.

DID YOU KNOW?

> Nowadays cosmetics experts advocate that substances to remove dead skin (exfoliants) should be used as little as possible, because ageing skin loses its thickness naturally and has no need of abrasive products. Modern research is concerned with prolonging the life of the cells in the corneum layer (outermost layer of the skin) by keeping them, and the substances that bind them, in place as long as possible.

> The hypodermic junction, the latest technological ally in the battle against ageing, involves stimulating

• **Ceramides:** these lipids retain moisture and stabilize the structure of the skin.
• **Collagen:** this excellent moisturizing agent has been used for a long time in the manufacture of cosmetics.
• **Elastin:** like collagen, this substance is naturally present in the skin and gives it its elasticity. When applied as a cream, its protein content encourages the formation of a moisture-retaining protective layer.
• **Enzymes:** these proteins, derived from certain plants, remove dead skin and, therefore, improve skin texture. They are less irritating than the AHAs.
• **Oxygen:** this has often been used in creams in recent years but its effectiveness as a cosmetic seems open to question.
• **Peptides:** these amino acids can boost the skin's secretory activity by stimulating the production of vital substances like collagen.

• **Tea:** thanks to antioxidant phenols, tea (especially green tea) is arousing more and more scientific interest. It can be found in various body creams.

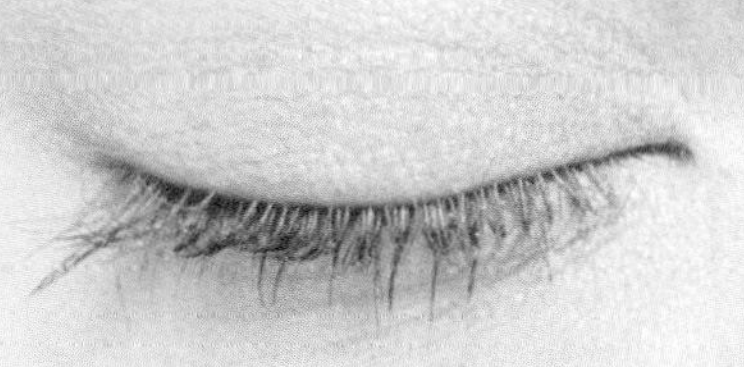

• **Vitamin A:** this is often combined with retinol (Retin-A) but can cause side-effects. Less powerful derivatives called retinyls are used in numerous anti-ageing creams.

the skin's self-defence systems with substances usually of plant origin, such as grape-seed, prickly pear, sunflower, apple and cabbage rose extracts, Grenoble walnut and freshwater blue algae. The list is a long one and is getting longer all the time.

KEY FACTS

* Nervous tension can accentuate wrinkles. Stay cool! Whilst on the subject, check out a new science called neurocosmetics.

* Don't use too much retinol – it may dry up the skin.

* Don't treat your skin with too many different active ingredients.

get your wrinkles under control

The first thing to do is to accept that wrinkles are there. The passage of time as well as past mistakes, such as too much sun, too many cigarettes and too much stress, have left their marks on you. Modern cosmetics won't make them disappear but will make them less obvious.

First rule: moisturize

Keeping your skin permanently moisturized is the key method of preventing wrinkles. It's no longer a question of buying anything that happens to be on the market. Only choose products specifically made for mature skin. In the mornings, apply a day protective cream (with ultraviolet screen) to your face, neck and shoulders. Make sure that the air in the rooms where you live is

DID YOU KNOW?

> The amount and depth of your wrinkles will depend on skin type, heredity, facial mannerisms, whether you smoke, but most of all, of course, on ultraviolet rays which affect the skin all the time, not only when you're sunbathing.

> Sunlight can damage the skin at any time of the year, even in the depths of winter and even through glass. In the summer apply a good sunscreen on all exposed parts (face, neck and shoulders, hands).

sufficiently moist: central heating and air conditioning are notorious for drying your skin. If necessary, buy a humidifier but make sure you disinfect it regularly to prevent bacteria.

Second rule: regenerate and stimulate

Ageing of the skin is probably due to over exposure to sunlight over the years. Night cream aims to repair the damage done during the day. Apply it after having carefully removed your make-up. Rub it in gently with your fingertips, using upwards circular movements. Do the same for your neck and shoulders but this time the movements should be downwards.

> In summer, get into the habit of wearing a straw hat (very trendy!), which will provide good protection for the face. Always carry a tube of sun block, so you can put some on your hands several times a day.

Third rule: don't frown!

An expressive face is certainly more attractive than a totally expressionless one. However, many of us have facial mannerisms that help to create deep lines on the forehead. Removing them isn't easy. Ask your friends and family to tell you every time you wrinkle up your face and try to treat yourself to a face massage every week at the beauty salon.

KEY FACTS

* For more radical skin care, use anti-ageing serum once a month.

* To smooth over your lines before an evening out, put on a face pack and lie down for 15 minutes.

* Choose a non-alcoholic toning lotion.

As you grow older, your face loses its firm shape. Just how it does so, depends on your skin type. Thin skins tend to wrinkle, whilst thick ones sag. But don't panic! Just tone up your face!

keep your face in good shape

Products to firm up your face

Skin toning products aim to stimulate the production of collagen, protect fibroblasts (cells in connective tissue responsible for producing fibres) from internal and external damage, boost blood flow and drain away toxins.
You'll find many such products in the shops. Their effect is usually indicated by their name, which must include such

DID YOU KNOW?

> Facial skin begins to lose its firmness, because the dermis (second layer of skin) has more and more difficulty in renewing damaged fibroblasts. As less and less collagen and elastin are produced, so the skin loses tone and elasticity. The dermis, a kind of mattress that the epidermis rests upon, begins to slacken and shrink. Add to this the slackening of the facial muscles, which are also subject to the law of gravity, and you'll understand why your whole face seems as if it's being irresistibly dragged down.

words as 'Lift', 'Firmness' and 'Firm'. Look closely at what is written on the packaging and go for well-known brands.

How to tone up your face

• Take the opportunity to massage in face cream by making little rising circular movements with your fingertips. To tone up the area around your lips, push your lips forward as if blowing into a trumpet and then purse them as if playing a flute.
• Keep your toning lotion and mineral water spray in the refrigerator. They'll be more effective.
• Avoid overheated rooms and sleep with a window open.
• Gently massage above and below the eyebrows, working from the nose outwards. This is guaranteed to drain the skin and relieve stress.

> The most effective anti-sagging products are those with a base of 'stapling' substances, which extend the time the dermis and epidermis remain bound together and also stimulate the renewal of cells.

KEY FACTS

* Ask a beautician to teach you the 'Jacquet pinchings'. This is when you pinch the skin firmly enough to tone up the epidermis (outermost layer of skin) but gently enough not to stretch it.

* Hold your head up to disguise a double chin.

24 try a face pack for a fresh, new look

A face pack is a gift to your skin, a rejuvenating treat that you can offer it when you have a little time just for yourself.

A precious moment of relaxation: a face pack will do you little good if you're stressed or in too much of a hurry. For maximum effect, give yourself at least 15 minutes of total relaxation. After you have carefully removed all make-up, apply an even layer of the face pack over your whole face, except your eyes. Then lie down, relax and read a magazine or listen to some soft music, your feet resting on a plump cushion. All the time you're putting on the pack, breathe deeply from the diaphragm. Afterwards you'll look great and feel refreshed and ready for anything!

Treat your breasts to a face pack: a face pack stimulates blood circulation and has a tightening effect on your skin. You might call it nature's bra. Apply it very gently, avoiding the area around the nipples. Leave it on for 15 minutes and then rinse off with cold water. Finally, spray on some flower water.

DID YOU KNOW?

> Choose the face pack specifically made for your problem: soothing to eliminate red blotches; toning for a tightening effect; cleansing to remove deep-seated impurities; anti-shine for greasy skins; refreshing and relaxing before an evening out.

KEY FACTS

* Always keep a variety of different face packs at home, ready for use whenever you feel the need.

* There are also packs to use on the hair.

25 preventing liver spots

The brown spots, which appear on the face, hands, neck and shoulders are caused by the cumulative effect of ultraviolet rays. It is never too late to prevent them or to try to limit the damage.

Protect yourself the whole year round! This can never be said too often – the sun affects our skin in winter as well as in summer. So get into the habit of protecting yourself all year round. Always put some sun block on your hands before going out. Keep a tube by the front door and another in the car for convenience. For your face and neck, choose moisturizing creams and make-up products, like foundation creams and tinted day creams, that include a sun block. Check the packaging to ensure it's there.

Consult a dermatologist: treatment with tretinoin (Retinova or Renova cream) can make liver spots much less obvious. Some doctors prescribe fruit acid, vitamin A acid and corticoid preparations to lighten liver spots. Don't hesitate to talk to your doctor about it.

DID YOU KNOW?

> Age/liver spots are caused by overactive melanocytes, the cells that produce melanin, the skin's natural pigment.

> People who have spent their summers in the sun are more affected than others.

KEY FACTS

* Heredity can also be held responsible for liver spots. Some skins seem predisposed to them, however little they are exposed to ultraviolet rays.

* It is possible to remove the spots with laser resurfacing or other techniques (see Tip 54).

As you get older, your lips get narrower and more pinched and the corners of your mouth tend inexorably to drop. It can make your face look unattractive but it is possible to avoid this happening.

take special care of your lips

Moisturizing and 'plumping'

Almost all women dream of having plump, fleshy lips that are for many the sign of sensuality. Before taking the plunge and having surgery, which you may later come to bitterly regret, try lip rejuvenating creams which have a visible 'plumping' effect and help to smooth out the fine lines around the mouth. You apply the creams on and around the lips.

DID YOU KNOW?

> The skin on the lips is in fact a mucous membrane. It is inevitably more fragile than the rest of the skin since it is composed of only five layers, compared with fifteen for the rest of the skin. What is more, it has an unfortunate tendency to crack. This often occurs in winter and could be due to cold weather and a shortage of vitamin D, caused by the lack of sunlight. If you suffer from cracked lips, talk to your doctor about it. He may prescribe you a dose of vitamin D.

Make-up tips

A typical problem when lips are not so young is that lipstick doesn't stay in place. As you get older, it tends to spread onto places where it shouldn't. The remedy is to draw a fine line around your mouth with a lip pencil before applying the lipstick. The wax in the pencil will prevent the lipstick from running. Avoid very dark shades, which tend to harden the face. As a general rule, choose one shade darker than the natural colour of your lips. Wear bright red lipsticks only when you're suntanned. Otherwise, choose pinkish or orangey shades. Ask your friends and family what they think. Lipstick is the item of make-up most obvious to the eye, so they are sure to have an opinion. And one final and important tip – check regularly to make sure your lipstick has not left any traces on your teeth!

> Always use a vitamin-enriched lip balm. Buy at least four sticks, so that you've always got one handy (in your handbag, in the car, at home and in your office drawer).

KEY FACTS

* To smooth out vertical lines around the mouth, apply a cream specially made for that particular area of the face mornings and evenings.

* Smile and laugh! It's the most effective way of combatting the mouth's natural tendency to sag.

Around the age of fifty it's common for women to want to change their hairstyle. Before having a revolutionary new cut or changing your hair colour, make sure you use some hair care products specially designed to cater for the changing needs of your hair.

take good care of your hair

Shiny hair is young-looking hair

As time goes by, hair tends to lose its shine, volume and resilience. Therefore, it's a good idea to choose a shorter style and to use products specially made for your age group that prevent hair loss and restore lustre and vitality. Among the treatments available, try those that contain natural substances like wheat-germ (which is nourishing), shea butter (which is conditioning), citrus fruit

DID YOU KNOW?

> The amount, strength and general quality of your hair is largely the result of hereditary factors. Some women will have beautiful hair all their lives, whilst others will have thin, fragile hair from childhood. On the other hand, since hair draws its energy from the capillaries on the scalp, its appearance is also influenced by diet. It requires vitamins (B, E and F), trace elements (zinc, selenium, sulphur, iron), mineral salts (magnesium, calcium) and amino acids.

(which contains vitamins), rhassoul (which has cleansing properties) and essential oils (for restoring hair balance). Vegetable substances are, in fact, more easily absorbed than chemical ones and penetrate the keratin in the hair more effectively. Every other weekend use a beauty mask on your hair designed to treat its particular problem. Leave it on for 20 minutes under a warm towel. You'll be astonished by the results, especially if you do it regularly.

If your hair is dyed or tinted

To protect your hair and revive its colour, always shampoo it with products which have a specific function. Apply a pre-shampoo to protect the pigments from water and detergent substances. Then use an ultra-gentle shampoo specially made for coloured hair. Finally, an after-shampoo conditioner will leave your hair smooth and shiny.

> Food supplements can be very useful if there is any shortage of these essential requirements. There are some that have even been specially devised to treat occasional hair loss. Some women experience hair loss after the menopause.

KEY FACTS

* You have about 120,000 hairs on your head and lose 30,000 per year, between 50 and 100 a day on average.

* The sun damages your hair, particularly from middle age onwards. Protect it by wearing a hat or a scarf.

28 introduce some colour

Grey hair suits some women, especially those who have had grey hair since they were quite young. However, when you're around the age of fifty, it nearly always puts years on you. So it's time to do something about it.

DID YOU KNOW?

> Grey hairs don't actually exist. They are an optical illusion caused by the close proximity of normally coloured and white hair.

An equal amount of the two colours produces the effect of beautiful, shiny, uniformly grey hair. Loss of hair colour is a gradual process which requires products adapted to each stage, as you reach it.

At the salon or at home?

To begin with, it's not a problem, because the first grey hairs can be removed with tweezers. This method can work well for a bit but, sooner or later, you'll have to give it up, because there'll be just too many grey hairs to deal with.

For a while, all you'll need is a colouring cream to hide the grey hairs without darkening the natural colour of the rest. You can get your hairdresser to do this or you can do it at home in less than an hour. Remember that from middle age onwards, colours that are too dark will tend to make you look older. Your main problem, therefore, is in choosing the right shade – it needs to be dark enough to conceal your grey hairs but light enough not to make your features look too harsh.

Different products

Temporary or semi-permanent colouring products are becoming more and more effective and easy to use but the colour will begin to fade after a certain number of hair washes. When, after a few attempts, you have found the right colour, you might feel confident enough to use two slightly different shades. If so, apply the lighter shade around your face to give your skin more colour. If your hair is predominantly grey, it's better to ask your hairdresser to give you a permanent colour, using stronger products that penetrate the sheath of the hair. Make sure you keep an eye on the roots though and take the necessary action as soon as they become noticeable.

> Besides shades that are too dark, avoid colouring that is too uniform, because it looks unnatural. You can have some highlights here and there but that is complicated work better done by a hairdresser.

KEY FACTS

* Choose shampoos and conditioners specially devised for dyed or coloured hair.

* Certain fifty-year-olds are tempted to try bright red shades, which the Italians call 'menopause red'. Be on your guard!

look after your eyes

Your eyes, and even more so their expression, are the first thing other people notice and they are one of your main assets. They are also the most delicate part of your face and deserve a lot of attention.

Smooth out wrinkles and crow's feet

You will not be able to avoid the fine lines that spread out from the corners of your eyes or the wrinkles underneath your eyes. They are caused by your facial expressions and, in particular, by laughing and smiling. You should learn to like them, because they are a reflection of your positive emotions, unlike the ugly lines on your forehead. You can, however, do something about the factors that make the situation worse like cigarettes, strong sunlight and stress. Always carry tinted glasses with you, so you never have to screw up your eyes against the sun. Nourish the area around your eyes with a special cream (ordinary face creams are too rich and aggressive). Apply it around the external corners in the mornings and evenings. Tap the cream gently in with your fingertips so that it penetrates. If you work in overheated or very dry premises, put some on at midday.

What to do about bags under the eyes

To a large extent bags under the eyes are hereditary, but bad diet and excessive alcohol can make the situation much worse. Don't eat too much Japanese and Chinese food as it contains high quantities of sodium glutamate (soya sauce is full of it) and, as a general rule, avoid eating too much salty food of any kind. To treat swollen eyes, try a cooling mask, which you can keep in the ice compartment of your refrigerator. Every morning, apply a gel specially made for the purpose.

DID YOU KNOW?

> The area around the eye is the part of the face that ages most rapidly. Our eyelids are a little like a butterfly's wings; they open and close 10,000 times a day and their skin is 10 times thinner than that on the rest of the face. So they need to be treated with the utmost care! Take two tea bags soaked in lukewarm water and then rung out, or two pieces of cotton wool soaked in ice-cold milk and then wrung out, or two little silk bags filled with sesame seeds, lie down and place them on your closed eyes. The weight on the eyelids allows the muscles in the eye socket to relax and gives the eyes a more rested appearance.

KEY FACTS

* Keep the cream you use around your eyes in the refrigerator. The cold helps to reduce the size of the bags.

* If you have bloodshot eyes, try some soothing eye drops.

* Conceal dark rings under your eyes with a tinted stick, made for the purpose, applied under your make-up.

keep your skin as smooth as a peach

Desire is aroused by sight and confirmed by touch. Having a soft, firm skin is vital if you want to remain attractive. Keeping a skin like velvet is far from impossible if you spend the necessary time on it.

A beautiful body is a well looked after body

Once you've passed fifty, a firm, smooth body is no longer something to be taken for granted but is the fruit of daily care and effort, which communicates your self-confidence to others. It is not a question of seeking an impossible perfection but of learning to love your body as it is now, whilst making every effort to improve it.

DID YOU KNOW?

> Exfoliation removes dead cells from the surface of the skin and, therefore, makes the skin more lustrous and soft. But don't overdo it. Just like facial skin, body skin loses thickness as we get older and exfoliants speed up the process.

> Thorough exfoliation when you get back from your summer holidays and again at the beginning of spring should be enough. The rest of the time, just keep on moisturizing!

A silky skin over firm muscles

Daily, or twice daily, moisturizing is the first act to include in your beauty ritual. Choose a rich, smooth, nourishing cream and massage it in until it has all been absorbed. If you have cellulite, apply an anti-cellulite cream (with a base of caffeine or cola) to the problem areas.
As for the areas that tend to slacken more quickly than the others (the inside of the arms and thighs, the buttocks and so on), treat them with a body 'lift' product and, of course, exercise as much as possible (see Tip 11)!
To consolidate the effect of these products, make your skin more supple and combat water retention, discover the benefits of the lymphatic stimulator – a sort of brush with thick rubber nodes. You brush your body with it every evening, starting from the soles of your feet and moving upwards. You do the same thing on your arms, starting from the palms. The movements must always be towards the heart. This treatment is also very relaxing and prepares you for sleep.

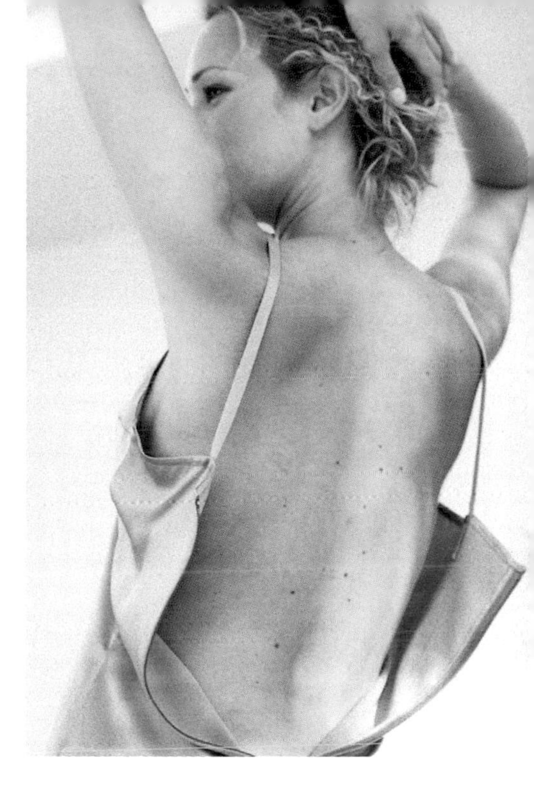

KEY FACTS

* Take the time to ensure that you have massaged in the cream completely.

* Don't forget your elbows! To prevent them from going dry, avoid leaning on them and treat them daily with a particularly nourishing cream.

Women tend to neglect their neck. This is a pity, because it often gives away their age more obviously than their face or body. Take an honest look at your neck and start to give it all the attention and special treatments it deserves.

don't neglect your neck

Always hold your head high

The neck has a distressing tendency to wrinkle. If you want to avoid being condemned to wearing collars, scarves and other means of concealment some years from now, begin by holding your head and your chin high. This will firm up the muscles of the neck and also prevent another widespread curse, the double chin.

DID YOU KNOW?

> Slimming regimes do nothing for your neck. Women who have lost a lot of weight or have lost it too quickly will bear this out. The loss of pounds or kilos, particularly a lot of pounds or kilos, is often paid for by a slack and wrinkled neck.

> The reason is obvious. The loss of fat 'empties' the neck, leaving the skin wrinkled and distended. This can happen at any age, and at yours in particular.

Daily exercises

Every morning do these exercises:
• keeping your shoulders still, turn your neck as far as you can so that you can see behind you (6 times to the left, 6 times to the right);
• tip your head backwards as if studying the ceiling. Hold the position for 2 seconds, then lower your head to touch your chest with your chin (10 times).
• keeping your shoulders still, swivel your head round without stopping (6 times from left to right, 6 times from right to left).

Massage and moisturize

Use a cream specially prepared for the neck, or a face cream rather than a body cream. Take the opportunity to give yourself a quick massage. Apply the cream with your fingertips using firm, circular and upward movements.

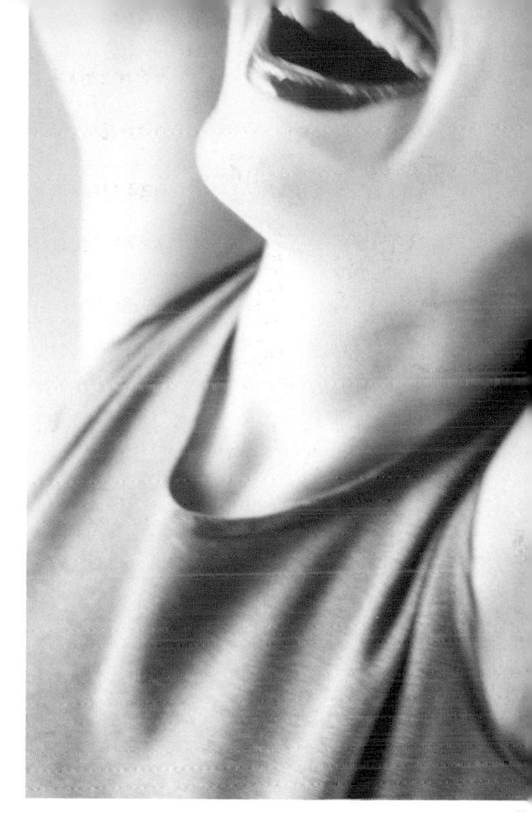

> It is very difficult to 'retighten' the neck without surgery, for it has very few muscles on which to work: one reason, among many, for avoiding very strict diets and for taking good care of your neck.

KEY FACTS

* The sun harms your neck more than anything else does. Never go out without first putting on sunscreen.

* Walking around like a queen is a great asset. Keep your head high and your neck straight.

32 avoid a distended stomach

Bloated stomachs are unattractive and, above all, painful. This problem, caused by what you eat and the way you eat it, tends to occur more often during the menopause.

Learn to chew again: if you eat too quickly, you're just asking for an upset stomach because the first phase of digestion has not been allowed to happen. The food arrives in the stomach inadequately broken down and without undergoing the chemical actions of the enzymes in the saliva. The stomach, therefore, has to use up more of its gastric juices to compensate. All of this gives rise to a series of adverse reactions: coated tongue, stomach acidity and, above all, flatulence, due to the formation of gas in the colon. Therefore, it is crucial to chew thoroughly, appreciating every mouthful and concentrating on the texture of the food as much as its taste.

Strengthen your abdominals: strong abdominal muscles are an excellent way of avoiding a bloated stomach. Do some strengthening exercises every morning.

DID YOU KNOW?

> Fibre in food can cause bloating. Don't eat too many raw vegetables; avoid peas and wholemeal bread; limit your intake of potatoes, wholewheat cereals, pulses, garlic and onions.

> Capsules with a base of charcoal, clay or fennel are good for curing this problem.

KEY FACTS

* People who eat alone are more liable to suffer from a bloated stomach: having no one to talk to, they can eat too quickly.

* If you suffer from bloating, lie down and massage your stomach with circular movements.

33 discover anti-ageing plants

Herbal medicine uses plants to cure illnesses. Unlike traditional (western) medicine, it does not rely upon a single, isolated active element but on the harmonious balance of several substances.

An update on plant hormones: some menopausal problems can be helped with plant hormones. Herbal oestrogens have qualities similar to hormones found in humans and could offer some relief from menopausal symptoms, such as flushing and sweats, with a lower risk of side effects.

The best-known hormones are isoflavones, which are extracted from soya. Asiatic women eat a lot of soya and experience far fewer menopausal disorders. Their cancer rates are much lower than ours too.

A herbal progesterone cream is obtained from the yam, a Mexican plant. It is said to give some relief to menopausal symptoms but absorption is patchy and not enough to give reliable protection against osteoporosis.

DID YOU KNOW?

> ***Panax ginseng*** **is an effective treatment for vaginal dryness, hot flushes, anxiety and palpitations.**

> ***Ginkgo biloba*** **stimulates hormonal activity and improves blood circulation.**

> **St John's wort can be effective in treating the symptoms of less severe forms of depression.**

KEY FACTS

* A mixture of sage, soya and evening primrose can reduce menopausal problems.

* Plant hormones such as progesterone creams from yams are favoured by some women.

Like your neck, your hands can mercilessly reveal your age. That's why, all year round, they require a lot of special attention. Once more, prevention is better than cure.

take care of your hands and nails

Four enemies that have to be overcome

• **Sunshine:** to prevent brown liver spots, always put sun block on your hands before going out. Keep several tubes or pots of it handy: in the hallway, the car, your office desk. Wear gloves when driving, to protect your hands from the sun.

• **The cold:** from the very first signs of winter, use a hand cream particularly

DID YOU KNOW?

> Although the palms have a thick protective layer of skin, the backs of the hands are covered with particularly thin skin with few sebaceous glands and have, therefore, little protection against the continuous damage inflicted by the outside world.

> The hands react to prolonged stress. It has been discovered that nervous tension, combined with the effects of cold and detergents, can be the cause of painful cracks around the nails.

rich in moisturizing agents. Never go out without gloves. If necessary, treat your hands to a 'mask': apply a thick layer of cream and then wear cotton gloves for an hour or two. A night at home in front of the television is an ideal time for this.

- **Detergents:** never wash dishes or clothes without wearing rubber gloves. You can buy very thin, supple ones.
- **Dryness:** wear thin cotton gloves when doing the housework because dust dries up the hands. If you handle large amounts of paper at work, put on cream during the day as paper absorbs the skin's natural moisture.

Keep an eye on your nails

Long nails may continue to attract some men but they do tend to make you look older. It's better to keep them quite short, cut squarish and impeccably filed. You need to inspect them every day. As for nail polish, forget about all the dark shades (brown, dark red, blue etc.) even if they are in fashion, because they're certain to make you look like a witch. Use transparent polish on a daily basis and keep colour for your evenings out on the town. Never use pearly nail polishes. They don't suit anyone and certainly not you.

> Because they are very often exposed to daylight, the hands are the first to suffer from brown liver spots. To keep them smooth and soft to the touch, they need daily care and totally reliable protection.

KEY FACTS

* There are some creams that will lighten the colour of skin blotches after 6 months of regular use.

* If your hands feel tense, massage them. Draw down on each finger in turn, then massage your hands with gentle, perfumed cream.

35 don't forget your feet

Do your feet feel a little tired? Considering all the time they have spent supporting the weight of your body, confined in shoes often too tight and seldom suited to their shape, it's not surprising that they're beginning to protest. It's time to give them a helping hand!

DID YOU KNOW?

> The foot, this mechanical masterpiece made up of 28 bones and 33 joints, tends to lose its shape when you get older.

> The most common problem is the hallux valgus (or bunion), a bony knob on the outside of the big toe, which can cause the big toe to overlap with the second toe.

A small problem, but a painful one

Corn, callosity, heloma: just reading these words makes you want to say, ouch! What is involved in all three cases is a small area of skin with a hard central core which presses upon the capillaries, often with acutely painful results. These discomforts are the result of the repeated rubbing of a shoe on certain parts of the foot. Corns are usually found on the top part of the toe, under the arch or between the toes. Moisture only makes the situation worse. To get rid of them, don't try self-medication or hacking them about at home – this could cause infections. Go to a chiropodist, who will remove them with a surgeon's knife. To prevent them developing, wear more comfortable shoes; dry your feet very, very carefully, taking care to dry between the toes with the corner of a towel; as often as possible, give your feet a chance to breathe by walking about the house in either sandals or socks, according to the weather.

> If this is happening to you, give up stiletto heels and tight-fitting shoes and wear toe separators and special soles. Walk barefoot as much as possible. Swivel your big toes around to loosen them up. If you are in pain, consider some laser treatment. There arc surgical treatments available that are quite successful.

If you've got an ingrown toenail, act immediately

This problem usually concerns the big toe: it becomes swollen, red around the nail and painful. Go immediately to the chiropodist, who will remove the ingrown part, clean the wound and ensure that the nail grows again without causing any further problems. If you wait too long, you run the risk of having to have real surgery.

KEY FACTS

* Far from being a luxury, a monthly visit to the chiropodist will save you a lot of trouble in the future… and you'll be able to continue to wear sandals in the summer.

* Without some pretty varnish on your toenails, your feet will never look really smart.

Make-up is one of your most powerful allies, so you must certainly not stop using it! However, the older you get, the less room there is for error. The time has come for you to review the make-up you have and to become a real expert.

update your make-up

Don't let long-sightedness be an obstacle

You must not stop using make-up on the pretext that you can't see as well. Get used to using a magnifying mirror when doing your face and your eyes, and then put on your glasses to correct any possible mistakes. Keep them on for making up your lips.

Foundation cream and blusher: use sparingly

• **Foundation cream:** replace with tinted moisturizing cream (with protection against ultraviolet rays).
• **Blusher:** choose orangey shades rather than bright reds but also avoid shades that are too dull. Using a brush, move from the centre of the cheek (on a level with the nostrils) up to the temple. Your features will seem to have been lifted upwards.

• **Face powder:** only use a very small amount, as it tends to accentuate wrinkles. Choose a powder that has none of the tones of your tinted cream. Apply with a large brush on the shiny areas only (point of the chin, nose, forehead). Buy a compact of the same powder for use during the day.

Be careful with the eyes!

• **Avoid at all costs:** liquid eye-liner, which hardens your expression and makes you look older; false eyelashes; too much mascara, which can go lumpy; eye shadows in shades of bright blue, light green and other loud colours. They didn't even suit you 25 years ago!

• **Use immediately:** a brown eye-shadow pencil to gently emphasize the outline of the eye; two or three coloured eyeshadows (dark olive green, brown, dark purple); pearly eyeshadow (white or pinkish) – dab little touches under your eyebrows when putting on your evening make-up.

DID YOU KNOW?

> Making up the lips is particularly tricky. You need to take into account the changes they have undergone over the years and correct them as discreetly as possible. Don't try to artificially enlarge the area of your lips: the result will be quite grotesque. Avoid smudges (see Tip 26).

> Forget deep colours such as brown, dark red etc. for your lips, unless you've chosen the vampire look. Depending on skin and hair colour, choose delicate reds, pinks or shades of terracotta. Outline the edges of your lips with a lip pencil before applying your lipstick or lip gloss, to prevent it from spreading.

KEY FACTS

* The key word is 'soften'. To achieve this effect use a cotton bud for the eyeshadow and eyelid pencil, cotton wool for the blusher and gently dab your lips with a paper tissue after putting on your lipstick.

* Your eyebrow line must be perfect. Look out for stray hairs.

make bathtime special

A long bath will wash away all the day's wear and tear. Anxiety, tension and negative feelings will disappear as if by magic in the hot, scented water. So in you go!

A few private moments all to yourself

Make a real ritual of bathtime. Take the phone off the hook and lock the bathroom door. Fill the bath with warm water and then pour in your favourite bath oil. Put on some soft music, light a candle or two and soak for 20 to 30 minutes with a little sponge cushion supporting the back of your head. You'll come out feeling as good as new.

DID YOU KNOW?

> Essential oils are the fragrant, volatile substances contained in what are known as 'aromatic' plants.

> Smells are stored in the same place in the brain as our long-term memory. That's why a mere whiff of scent can remind us of a happy moment.

> Primitive man's sense of smell was very acute, enabling him to detect the approach of an enemy.

> By pouring twenty or so drops of essential oil into your daily bathwater, you will gradually rediscover the potential of your sense of smell.

Bath oils to meet your various needs

It has been proved that aromatic oils have positive effects on the nervous system. Pour 20 to 30 drops into your bath and stir the water well, because they don't dissolve easily.

• To get rid of all the wear and tear of the day: essential oil of lavender, camomile, marjoram or lemon balm.
• To feel full of energy before going to work: peppermint, anise and cinnamon.
• To boost your intellectual capacity: clove, thyme or basil.

How to really enjoy your bath

• Relax blissfully for at least 5 minutes.
• Using a brush with a handle, rub your body making circular movements. Start from your feet and go up to your neck. Then brush your arms, starting from your hands and working upwards. Stand up in the bath, brush behind your legs and then your buttocks and your back.
• Try out some stretching exercises (see Tip 9).
• Rinse yourself with fresh water.
• Slip on a towelling dressing gown that has been warming on the radiator and dry yourself carefully.
• Moisturize your skin deeply with a body cream.

KEY FACTS

* Don't use gels too often. Choose oils, salts and sea algae instead.

* Try a herbal tea bath. Empty five sachets of mint, camomile or lime tea onto a large, square piece of gauze. Fold and tie up with string and hold under the tap while the water is running.

Modern farming techniques destroy some of the nutrients in our food. The menopause itself tends to cause some shortages so it can be necessary to take supplements to compensate, but do try to eat a healthy, mixed diet.

finding out about food supplements

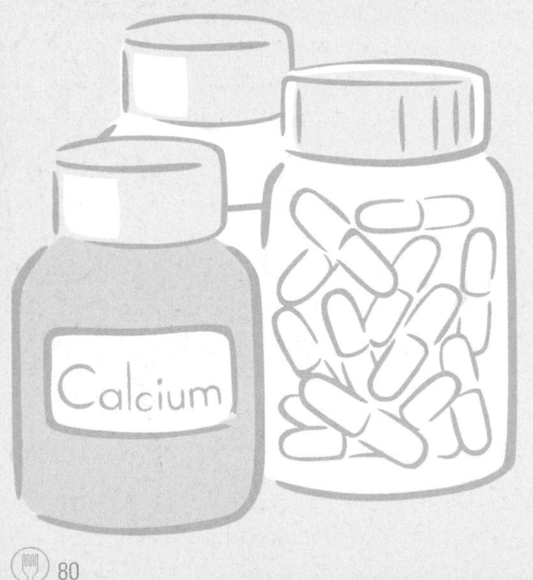

Consult your doctor

Above all, don't prescribe food supplements for yourself. Only a blood test can establish whether you are suffering from shortages and, if so, only a doctor will be able to prescribe the doses that you really need. If you smoke or drink a lot of alcohol, tell him/her, because in that case you will require higher doses.

Anti-ageing supplements:

• **vitamin A:** an antioxidant that improves quality of the skin, strengthens the immune system and reduces cell degeneration.
• **vitamin C:** this strengthens the body's defence systems, combats stress and tiredness, protects against some cancers, permits the formation of collagen and

helps in the absorption of iron and calcium. All women over fifty ought to take a supplement of at least 1mg per day.

- **zinc:** an excellent antioxidant. It strengthens the immune system and protects the skin, bones and genes.
- **selenium:** supplements are recommended if you smoke, drink a lot and have a large number of dental fillings.
- **calcium:** this must be combined with magnesium and should be taken at several intervals, so that it is not passed out in the urine.
- **vitamin E:** combats free radicals and can help prevent heart disease as well as certain cancers, including cancer of the colon.
- **vitamin Q (or co-enzyme Q10):** protects the nerve cells, helps to prevent gum diseases and has considerable antioxidant properties.
- **polyphenols:** the best-known are the flavenoids. It seems certain that they combat ageing thanks to their effects on blood circulation.

DID YOU KNOW?

> Essential fatty acids, including Omega 3 and 6, have become the stars of anti-ageing. Consider supplements if you have dry skin, are subject to allergies or suffer from high blood pressure or chronic viral infections, like herpes. Omega 3 fatty acids must always be combined with vitamin E to protect against oxidation.

> Oily fish (such as herring, salmon, tuna, sardines, and anchovies) are very important sources of these fatty acids, as is fish liver. Fatty acids can also be found in the outer skin of prawns.

> You can also supplement your intake by taking oil of evening primrose, borage oil, marrow seed or cold water fish capsules.

KEY FACTS

* You need between 400-800 units of vitamin D daily.

* If you are using supplements you may be getting your vitamins from several sources.

At about the age of fifty small-breasted women get some revenge, because they are less affected by the effects of the law of gravity. However, everyone's breasts lose some tone and shape.

keep your breasts looking beautiful

Tone up and nourish your breasts

To tone up your breasts, do as our grandmothers did: spray them with cold water under the shower for 2 minutes twice a day.

The skin on the breasts has very few sebaceous glands, so they should be nourished with moisturizing cream every day. There are creams specially made for the breasts. Try them but don't expect miracles.

DID YOU KNOW?

> Age, a succession of slimming diets and pregnancies are the main reasons for the breasts' loss of tone.

> Take advantage of the latest technology and choose a bra that is best suited to your particular needs.

> Small breasts are particularly well looked after nowadays. New adjustable 'push-up' bras are available, with cups filled with air, gel or water, which means everyone can display a swelling cleavage.

Strengthen your pectorals

The breasts contain no muscles, only a more or less developed mammary gland surrounded by body fat. The only way of improving their tone and shape is to strengthen the pectoral muscles that support them. You can do the necessary exercises either in a gym using special equipment or at home, as follows:

• sitting or standing, put the palms of your hands together as if you are praying. Push your elbows out level with your breasts and press your hands together hard, as if you're trying to crush something. (10 times in succession, twice a day).

• Lie on your back, knees bent and feet on the ground. Cross one foot over the opposite knee and lift your outstretched arms above your face while holding a large plastic bottle full of water. Breathe in and stretch your arms out behind your head. Breathe out and bring your arms back to the starting position above your face (repeat 20 times).

Do an hour's swimming twice a week. The breaststroke is very good exercise for the pectorals.

Always wear a suitable bra. Finally, pull your stomach in and push your chest out! That's the best way to show them off to advantage.

KEY FACTS

* Never expose your naked breasts to the sunlight. Quite apart from the question of appearance, it is dangerous: the free radicals generated by ultraviolet rays can cause skin cancers.

* Hormone Replacement Therapy (HRT) can keep your breasts looking shapely.

40 wage war on cellulite

Cellulite affects a lot of women whatever their age. However, if you're not careful, you'll get more of these ugly lumps of fat when you are menopausal. Resist their attacks!

You need to know your enemy before you can pursue it: cellulite consists of accumulations of fat and water on the thighs, hips, buttocks and stomach. To stop these liquids from gathering, the circulation of blood and lymph fluid needs to be improved. There are several available treatments: the new slimming creams, massage, physical exercise and specially devised diets.

A new generation of cosmetics: to reduce fats, two substances are thought to be vital – AMPC and the very new GMPC, extracted from geranium. There is also a new type of caffeine, which, when combined with protamine sulphate, is thought to be able to regulate the creation of new fats. Other products use Asiatic plants, tea, soya and wheatgerm oil.

DID YOU KNOW?

> There is nothing better than massage, either in a beauty salon or at home, for dealing with cellulite. Work on the critical areas every day with a lymphatic stimulator or other manual equipment available in specialist shops.

KEY FACTS

* Try not to wear anything that could impede the circulation, such as belts, tight-fitting boots and jeans.

* Avoid rich sauces, fried fish, cooked meats and any animal fats.

case study

Always looking great, thanks to anti-ageing creams

In the retail trade you mustn't look your age or look tired at the end of the afternoon. I've tried various lines of anti-ageing products. They're all useful, but it's important to find the one that suits you the best, because everybody's skin has its own special needs. Every Saturday evening I put on a relaxing face pack before going out. Every morning I apply a fruit acids moisturizing cream, a cream for the area around the lips and one for around the eyes. I also take these to work with me, to put on when necessary, because air conditioning dries up the skin. All day at work I wear special tights which stimulate blood circulation, to avoid the leg problems that are the curse of our profession, and I drink mineral water rich in calcium throughout the day. I treat myself to a visit to a good hairdresser once a month, so that my hairstyle and hair colouring are always looking great.

»» A healthy lifestyle, cosmetics specially made for your age group and a new attitude to yourself are 'musts' if you are to **approach the fifty year old mark without worries.** All the same, there will be no shortage of physical and psychological changes when your ovaries stop functioning.

»»»» Some women can **go to a specialist for help** or consider whether to have cosmetic surgery; others feel that new drugs and remedies are the answer.

»»»»»» Let's take stock, whilst **never forgetting that maturity will only be fulfilling if you accept it**: no surgery or chemical product can change that.

60
TIPS

make a new start

The human female is unique amongst living creatures: she is the only female who will probably live a third of her life when no longer capable of conception. Once freed from reproduction, she can build herself a new life.

A different generation of women

The menopause is indeed a physiological earthquake. The enormous hormonal changes have innumerable effects on the female organism, quite apart from the ageing process common to both sexes. Up until the preceding generation of women, the menopause meant the start of old age. But the arrival en masse of the female baby boomers at this landmark has changed the situation. You

DID YOU KNOW?

> The menopause is a natural part of life, just like puberty or maternity, but yet for a long time it was a subject hardly ever talked about. Many divorces take place around this time, the main reason being a lack of communication.

> Talking about this period of change to those close to you will enable them to understand you better and therefore respect you. Incidentally, women who have a worthwhile job or an absorbing leisure interest, find the menopause a better experience.

might not think it but you are transforming the way society considers women who are no longer fertile. Thanks to the wonderful progress of medical science and your generation's own special outlook on life, you can stay physically attractive, professionally active and in excellent health for many years to come...and you have an invaluable extra asset: experience of life and the wisdom this brings.

On the way downhill? Perhaps, but you've still got a lot of life left in you

The menopause used to be called the 'change of life'. In fact, it's more like a very important turning point. Being around the age of fifty is one of the most important times of your life with undeniable advantages. For the first time you are faced with an almost unlimited number of possibilities. A new journey awaits you: have a great trip!

> Do some further reading about the menopause – there are several useful websites you can check out.

KEY FACTS

* The age you are when your menopause starts is often the result of heredity.

* If your mother or an older sister had an early, or late, menopause, it is likely that you will have one too.

think seriously about HRT

Hormone Replacement Therapy provides the body with the oestrogens and progesterone that the ovaries have stopped producing and so reduces most of the symptoms caused by this shortage of hormones.

Some definite benefits and some possible ones

Hormonal Replacement Therapy (HRT) can put an end to hot flushes almost instantly; it restores energy, improves mood and reduces insomnia; in 80% of cases it combats loss of bone density and helps to prevent osteoporosis: it relieves joint pains, helps to control weight gain and maintain muscle mass.

●●● DID YOU KNOW?

> To be sure you're making the right decision, discuss it with your doctor or gynaecologist. Beware of those who advocate HRT no matter what and those who are totally against it. Make sure that he/she is really listening to you and taking account of your individual needs.

> Before prescribing HRT your doctor will confirm the diagnosis and perform tests if necessary. He/she will want to find out about your own medical history as well as your family history (in particular, any incidence of breast cancer).

In addition, HRT can also prevent Alzheimer's disease as well as improve memory and concentration difficulties.

The disadvantages

HRT can increase the risk of breast cancer. There is also a small definite increase in deep vein thrombosis and pulmonary embolism. The other disadvantages are less serious: weight gain, water retention (oedema), tension or pain in the breasts (but only if the product is not administered in the right doses); frequent periods.
Remember that you must have breast screening every two years if you present no risk factor or symptoms (pains, lumps etc.). If you are between 50 and 60/65 years old in the UK, for example, there is a nationwide breast screening programme. If you have a strong family history of cancer you should take appropriate advice from your GP, who may refer you to a specialist clinic.

KEY FACTS

* You can now take oestrogens by using tablets, patches, gels or a nasal spray – all available on prescription only.

* Find out about your local breast screening programme.

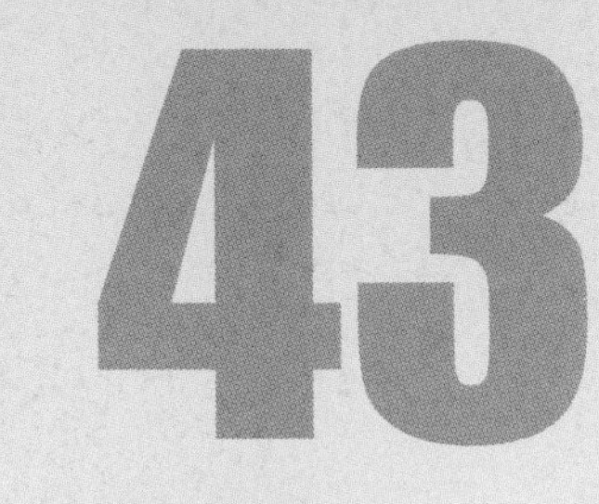

43 avoiding problems

Slowly but surely the risk of heart disease increases after the menopause. The risk is greater if you smoke, take little exercise, if your parents had heart problems, if you don't eat healthily and if you're often stressed.

●●● DID YOU KNOW?

> Before the menopause, women are four times less likely to suffer a heart attack than men. This is due to natural protection provided by oestrogen hormones, which widen the arteries and tend to reduce the level of bad cholesterol. This advantage lasts for some time after the ovaries have stopped functioning but then gradually disappears. At around the age of 60 there is no longer any difference between the sexes.

Hardening of the arteries, a disease lying in wait

This condition is the main cause of cardio-vascular illnesses. It results from the oxidation of blood fats, which form deposits on the artery walls. The walls then become thicker and more rigid and hinder blood circulation. Complete blockage of the artery leads to a blood clot and a heart attack. You need to take steps now to stop this from happening.

Exercise: your number one ally

A regular and sustained programme of exercise lowers the heart rate, may help to reduce 'bad' cholesterol and reduces the risk of a heart attack by 50%. When you are 50 you should do 1 hour of exercise/sport 3 times a week. At 60 you should change to 45 minute sessions 4 or 5 times a week. You should exercise less intensively as you get older but to make up for this, gradually increase the frequency of the sessions.

Copy the Cretans

The record life expectancy of the Cretans and their remarkably low level of heart disease have prompted many scientists to study their eating habits. These islanders consume no dairy products, except a little cheese, and very little meat and eggs. Their staple diet consists of pulses, pasta, couscous, rice and wholemeal bread: plenty of fruit and vegetables (including garlic and, above all, purslane, which has remarkable qualities); red wine at meals; and finally a lot of cagouilles (Cretan snails).

> Food supplements can provide very effective protection. Folic acid, vitamin E, which protects the artery walls (and is not at all toxic), magnesium and potassium, the Q10 co-enzyme, vitamins A and C and Omega-3 fatty acids are the ones to choose.

KEY FACTS

* Garlic is very good for the heart. One or two cloves a day will reduce the risk of a heart attack by 66%.

* Tea (green, oolong or black) prevents thromboses and reduces the levels of cholesterol and triglycerides.

a survey of new drugs

There has been a lot of talk for quite some time about synthetically produced hormones, particularly DHEA, which have become all the rage in France. Whichever one you may be considering, it pays to be careful.

Hormones, the source of youthfulness

These substances, which are vital to our well-being and health, affect the whole body. As we grow older, we produce less of them. This happens gradually, except during the menopause when it happens very suddenly. Synthetic hormones restore certain youthful properties to the body or at least enable us to grow old looking and feeling younger.

DID YOU KNOW?

> The cosmetic industry is becoming more and more interested in using new drugs, particularly synthetic hormones, in their anti-ageing products.

> However, you need to be very careful. When applied to the skin, DHEA penetrates directly into the bloodstream and, therefore, the possibility of side effects cannot be excluded.

DHEA under close scrutiny

DeHydroEpiAndrosterone stimulates the production of other hormones, such as oestrogens and androgens and has caused a lot of controversy. It seems more effective when used by the over 65's and unnecessary for women aged about 50 who are on HRT. People in the early stages of cancer must certainly not take this drug. It is not used in the UK.

Melatonin regulates the biological clock but...

Although effective as a way of combatting jet lag, this hormone's ability to slowdown ageing is yet to be proved. Nevertheless, many Americans have been taking it for years, convinced that it is a genuine elixir of youth.

Human growth hormone

A shortage of human growth hormone causes premature ageing. This gave rise to the idea of administering some to 'rejuvenate' elderly patients. The results seem convincing but there are significant side effects, such as water retention, diabetes and the risk of developing cancerous cells.

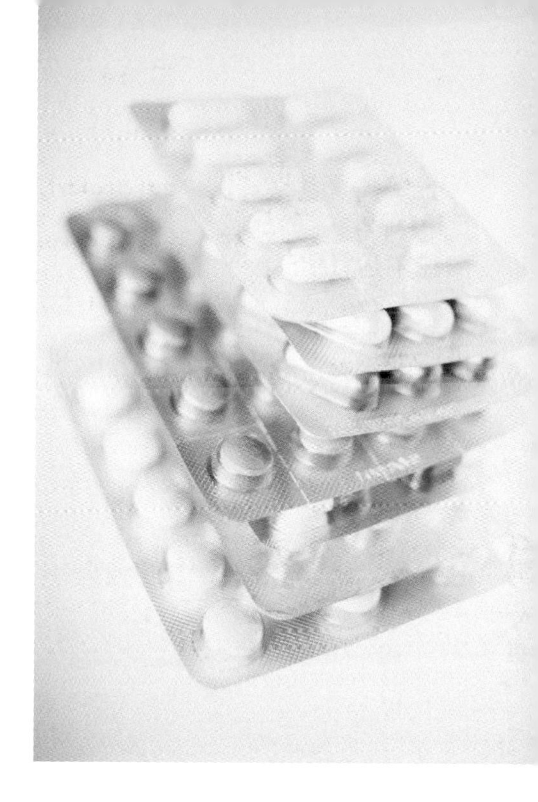

KEY FACTS

* Be careful! DHEA can easily be bought on the Internet. However, you should only obtain it from a pharmacy with a doctor's prescription.

* We won't know whether DHEA has worked or not on a 40 year old, until he/she has reached 80.

Face-lifts are the most common form of cosmetic surgery. The operation is not without its risks and could lead to a series of further operations. Don't make a hasty decision.

don't rush into having a face-lift

What does it involve exactly?

The surgeon cuts the skin and pulls the superficial muscle tissues upwards and backwards. He then removes the excess skin. The operation is usually performed under a general anaesthetic or, sometimes, under a local anaesthetic combined with a high dose of tranquillizers. It lasts between two and a half to four hours and you need to stay in hospital for at least 24 hours. After the operation

DID YOU KNOW?

> It is important to choose a surgeon you have confidence in. The best method of finding one is by word-of-mouth: you'll feel confident about a surgeon who has successfully lifted the face of one of your friends. Talk to two or three of them before making up your mind.

> Thanks to 'morphing' (a computer simulation of your face after the face-lift), you'll be able to get quite an accurate idea of the final result of the operation.

your face will be swollen, bruised, painful and stiff. If all goes well, your face will heal after about a month. The scars are hidden by your hair and ought to be after two months.

The results

A successful face-lift will make you look ten years younger and will remain noticeable for eight to ten years. After that, you will either have to resign yourself to your appearance or have another lift. If, however, it does not work, you'll have suffered for nothing and thrown your money away. Also, what's the use of having a smooth face if your hands are spotted and your muscles and breasts are sagging? Remember that youthfulness begins in the head. No face-lift will rejuvenate a woman who has no outside interests and is totally preoccupied by her daily routine.

> But don't forget that the best face-lift in the world won't guarantee the return of an erring husband, the arrival of the lover of your dreams or professional success ... and its effects aren't permanent.

KEY FACTS

* The average age for a first face-lift is 45 to 50.
* Plan to take some time off work after the operation: you won't be presentable for around a fortnight!
* Endoscopic face-lifting is a smaller operation. It is most suited to more supple and, therefore, younger skins.

There are other methods apart from a face-lift to restore firmness and tone to your face and remove or reduce wrinkles and lines.

46 alternatives to face-lifts

Firm up your skin with laser treatment

A new laser treatment, involving no removal of tissue, stimulates the natural production of collagen and fibroblasts by heating the dermis (second layer of skin) without affecting the epidermis (top layer). There are no post-operative effects, so you can return to your normal routine the day after the session (usually three are needed, one per month). You

●●● DID YOU KNOW?

> You can also smooth out your lines with a mask combined with vitamin A acid, which will stimulate your production of collagen. After putting on a whole tube of vitamin A acid, a hot mask is applied so that the substance can penetrate deeply.

> You are advised to have six masks (one a fortnight), then a monthly consolidation session for three months, followed by a mask every two or three months.

can also combine this therapy with a chemical peel using glycolic acid or alumina crystals. The only disadvantage is that the possibility of side effects cannot be ruled out, because this is such a recent technique.

Microinjections and mesolifting (mesotherapy).

• **Microinjections:** remedial substances are injected directly into the wrinkles. The substances used are hyaluronic acid (absorbent; its effect lasts for 9-12 months and botox frequently used for smoothing out lines on the forehead (non-degradable). Botox is based on the botulinum toxin and produces a temporary paralysis of the muscles that cause wrinkling. Three sessions are needed in the first year and two in the second.

• **Mesolifting or revitalization from the inside:** instead of injecting specific wrinkles, this therapy involves a large number of superficial injections of a gel with a base of hyaluronic acid into the dermis of a whole area of the face. An electronic pistol syringe is used for the purpose. This restores tone and suppleness to the tissues (four sessions – once a fortnight – then three sessions a month). The results last longer than microinjections.

Cryosculpture or cold therapy

This technique combines the use of electrical waves and freezing to help injected remedial substances to penetrate.

> When it comes to chemical peeling and dermabrasion (see Tip 54), be careful: facial scrubs can weaken the defence systems of mature skin. The more active the product is, as in the case of vitamin A acid, the higher the risk.

KEY FACTS

* These procedures are very expensive because they require several sessions.

* The risk of rejection or allergic reactions to these substances is very small but it is a factor to be taken into account.

consider eyelid surgery

Blepharoplasty or eyelid surgery involves a very delicate operation. It can be combined with endoscopic lifting of the upper face.

Above the eye: getting rid of that heavy fold! The aim is to 'open' the eye by cutting into the eyelid's natural fold in order to remove excess skin and fat. The scars are not visible. This procedure is often combined with botox injections to relax the muscles and prevent them from contracting. The operation lasts 1-2 hours under a local anaesthetic. You need to stay in hospital from 6-12 hours.

Below the eye: removing the fatty bags. Bags under the eye are often hereditary and quite ugly. The surgeon will remove the fat and will often push a part of it down to fill the depression below the bag. He will get rid of excess skin by making an incision level with the eyelashes. The length of the procedure and the time spent in hospital are the same as for the upper eyelid.

DID YOU KNOW?

> It is possible to smooth out the eyelids and crow's feet with Derma K laser treatment, which can also remove bags without scars and with less bruising. It avoids 'the cocker spaniel effect' – round, vacant eyes – caused by surgery that is not delicate enough.

KEY FACTS

* You will need to wear dark glasses for ten days.

* Dark rings around the eyes can be treated with hyaluronic acid. The effect lasts for 7-8 months.

48 get rid of your double chin

A double chin is definitely unattractive and puts years on you. You can make it disappear and, if you wish, tighten the skin on your neck at the same time.

Endoscopy, an ultramodern technique: the surgeon makes a tiny incision below the chin and inserts an endoscope with a micro-camera linked to a screen on which he can check everything he is doing. He then introduces through other tiny incisions endodissectors, minuscule instruments with which he can get rid of the surplus fat. This modern technique enables the surgeon to touch only the part of the face he needs to.

Liposuction with ultrasound: the fatty cells are liquified and then sucked up through cannulas. This procedure takes place under local anaesthetic and there is no need to spend time in hospital. It is best suited to skin that is sufficiently elastic to be able to retract by itself. The final result is discernible around three weeks afterwards.

DID YOU KNOW?

> When you reach 50, your neck sometimes poses problems (see Tip 31). If you can't bear yours anymore, endoscopic procedures on both double chin and neck are available.

> The surgeon will use the incisions made for the double chin and keep scarring to a minimum.

KEY FACTS

* The endoscopic procedure can be performed on both neck and double chin.

* After the operation, which is usually carried out under local anaesthetic, there can be a feeling of tightness in the area concerned.

As you grow older, your lips tend to become thinner. However, this is not sufficient reason to have your mouth reshaped. Excessively 'pumped up' lips can ruin your face. Take a good look around you before making up your mind.

49 reshaping your lips – think twice

Don't underestimate the risks

Lip surgery is far from being a small matter, as mistakes can cause you to smile permanently, prevent you from smiling properly in the first place or paralyse the muscles around the mouth. Some people find it hard to control their lips and have difficulty eating and drinking in public if the procedure is not successful.

DID YOU KNOW?

> If, despite everything, you want your mouth reshaped, there are different techniques to choose from.

- Lip lifting: the upper lip is lifted by removing a strip of skin from an area level with the nose.
- Implants: a little, non-absorbent tube made of biocompatible polymer is inserted around the lips.
- Injections of various products: New-fill, which is extracted by means of a surgical thread; Artecoll, used for correcting wrinkles; Dermalive for smoothing over

A spoiled mouth compromises the appearance of the whole face

Badly reshaped 'bee-stung' lips have been all the rage in magazines and in the media. Everyone is aware of how many highly attractive women who, for reasons as mysterious as they are worrying, have decided to have their lips altered. Fortunately, the craze for enormous mouths seems to been dying down. Far too many errors have meant that surgeons are no longer going to extremes. Nowadays, the argument is no longer about the risks attached to the products used, which are very much better regulated than they once were, but in the skill and the care of the surgeons themselves. Take great care when choosing your surgeon!

The natural shape must be preserved

Insist on this above all else. Numerous surgeons tend to choose the easy option by repeating stereotypical shapes, which they can do easily, without taking into account the specific features of their patient's face. 'Morphing' prior to the operation is recommended.

depressions in the outline of the lips; Perlane for smoothing wrinkles; Restylane for smaller, finer lines.

> The corners of the mouth can also be drawn upwards by making slight incisions in them. The result: a permanent smile like a doll.

KEY FACTS

* A single session of injections is generally not enough. To get a satisfactory effect, two or three are necessary.

* Prices vary depending on the procedure. Do some research.

should you consider breast surgery?

The passing of time, pregnancies and breastfeeding all take their toll on the breasts and the temptation to have tired breasts enlarged or lifted is perfectly understandable. However, before having this done, you must carefully weigh up the pros and the cons.

The different kinds of operation

• **Breast implants.** They can increase the size of breasts made too small by shrinkage of the mammary gland (due to the shortage of oestrogen) or a large weight loss. The implants are silicon envelopes filled with physiological saline that the surgeon inserts through an incision in the crease under the arms (axillary) or under the nipple area

DID YOU KNOW?

> The number of cosmetic breast operations being performed each year is steadily increasing. The results are often excellent. When the scars are under the armpits, they are invisible to the naked eye.

> However, it is not advisable to have round, erect breasts if the insides of your arms are wrinkled and sagging and your neck is not looking good. Above all else, beauty is a question of harmony, so beware of contrasts that ruin the effect.

(periareolar). They can be placed under or above the pectoral muscle, as required. The entire operation takes around one hour to one hour thirty minutes and you will need to spend 24 hours in hospital.

• **Lifting.** Sagging breasts can be lifted by the removal of excess skin. The incision is made just under the nipple area with the possibility of a vertical cut into the mammary fissure. If necessary, implants can also be placed behind the pectoral muscle. The operation takes from two hours to two hours thirty minutes and you will have to spend from 24 to 48 hours in hospital.

What are the risks?

There is a 2% chance of implant rejection. The scar tissue thickens, hardens and presses against the implant. The problem varies from an excessive hardness, which the surgeon can often reduce with massage, to a misshaping of one or both breasts, which requires another operation. In 1% of cases an implant swells and causes one breast to be bigger than the other.

KEY FACTS

* After the operation you'll need to wear a medical bra for a month.

* The breasts reach their permanent size one month after the operation.

* When the scars are under the armpit, they will be well concealed.

51 loss of libido? – don't despair

At midlife, sex can cause problems for some women. But it's not a disaster: there's a remedy for everything and your partner has an important role to play as well.

Reject old prejudices: some of us inherit, usually unconsciously, taboos, often deeply rooted in culture. Sex no longer linked with procreation is considered 'bad', almost 'against the law of nature'. It's time to be aware of these taboos and, in the apt words of the gynaecologist David Elia, not to let yourself be conditioned by horrible descriptions of vaginal atrophy and total loss of desire. There can be problems but they are quite treatable.

Vaginal dryness is not inevitable: this can happen 12 to 36 months after your last period, because of the lack of oestrogens, and causes pain and a burning sensation during sexual intercourse. HRT, applied in the form of a cream containing oestrogen, usually deals with the problem. If it persists, try lubricants, which can be bought in pharmacies without a prescription.

DID YOU KNOW?

> The decline of sexual desire springs from a number of factors, including a reduction of male hormones, hot flushes, tiredness and a partner's erection difficulties.

> A good discussion about the situation with your partner can solve all problems.

KEY FACTS

* Testosterone can be combined with HRT to revive the libido.

* Many menopausal women continue to have a satisfying sex life.

52 try contact lenses

If you really can't get used to glasses, you can try contact lenses for the longsighted: they are becoming more and more effective.

Who are they recommended for? The chronically absent-minded, who regularly forget or lose their glasses; the inveterately appearance- conscious, who can't bear to see themselves in specs; those who don't want to reveal their age by putting on reading glasses; those whose work requires them to make frequent appearances in public.

How much would you have to spend? You can choose between lenses you throw away every month and those you can keep for a year. You need to add to that the cleaning product and a good pair of glasses, necessary in case of loss, eye irritation or other problems.

What to avoid when wearing lenses: powerful air conditioning; very windy places; places filled with steam like saunas and steam baths.

DID YOU KNOW?

> You will certainly need to consult an ophthamologist, who will give you an examination to ensure that your secretion of tear fluid is adequate and that your eyes will suffer no side effects.

> No worthwhile optician will sell you contact lenses without asking to see a prescription.

KEY FACTS

* Lenses have to be kept scrupulously clean.

* You need time to adapt to contact lenses: there's a three month trial period before you have to make up your mind.

invest in your teeth and gums

Yellowing teeth and receding gums (which cause teeth to work loose) come with age and affect men as much as women. For those who have the means however, modern dentistry can solve these problems.

Teeth as white as snow

To regain the dazzling smile you had when you were 20, there are various options open.

- **Gutter splints:** these are plastic casts, onto which a gel with a base of hydrogen peroxide is applied. They are worn at night for two or three weeks and your tooth enamel is bleached.
- **Bleaching with a lamp:** the same gel is applied to the teeth, which are then

DID YOU KNOW?

> Receding gums can be hereditary and, if so, there is little that can be done. The problem can also be caused by lack of dental hygiene, because the formation of tartar on the teeth loosens the gums. It is therefore important that you visit your dentist regularly and have the tartar removed.

> Bacterial infections caused by inadequate cleaning can inflame the gums, which swell and no longer stick to the surface of the teeth. Vigorous brushing can also damage gum tissue, causing it to retract, so do take care.

heated with a plasma lamp to increase the product's effect. This technique can be combined with wearing plastic casts coated with hydrogen peroxide.

• **Facettes/veneers:** this procedure is used on the twelve teeth visible when we smile and involves a fine film (or veneer) made of porcelain or resin being stuck onto their surfaces. Firstly, the dentist, having administered a local anaesthetic, removes a very small amount of enamel with a special drill. He then puts the made-to-measure veneers on the teeth, whilst heating them with a lamp. The cost of porcelain and resin veneers will vary, so check with your dentist and do some research.

Receding gums: act without delay

If your gums are 'drawing back' and gradually revealing the roots of your teeth, you need to get treatment as soon as possible. Depending on the circumstances, the dentist will either simply pull the gum back to its original position or he/she will have to graft on tissue taken from the palate (some use biocompatible, non-absorbent materials like Gore-Tex instead). The operation lasts for about an hour and the stitches are removed after a week.

KEY FACTS

* To keep your teeth shiny after bleaching, use a calcium peroxide toothpaste. Have regular lamp sessions with your dentist.

* Good dental hygiene helps prevent peridontal disease – brush and floss after each meal.

* The cost of porcelain or resin veneers will vary, so check with your dentist.

54 removing imperfections

Used by themselves or in conjunction with cosmetic surgery, laser and peeling techniques can smooth away many imperfections. These are not, however, trivial procedures, so, once again, the matter needs to be approached with great care.

DID YOU KNOW?

> You can also remove brown age spots and lines by means of peeling or dermabrasion. In the first method, chemicals such as glycolic or trichloracetic acid are used, while in the second, the face is smoothed with a sort of diamond tipped 'sanding' device. The procedure is always preceded by a month's application of colour removing products and vitamin A cream.

How does the miracle ray work?

The laser is a destructive ray of light that strips off scales of skin by evaporating the water in the skin's cells. It stimulates the production of collagen and has a slight tautening effect because it retracts the tissues. Once you have been equipped with protective glasses for your eyes, the practitioner passes a kind of pencil, which emits the beam, over the area to be treated. He/she follows this with the aid of a computer and varies the power of the ray and the depth of the treatment according to the condition of the inner skin layers, which are displayed on the screen. After the session, the area will be red and covered in little scabs. It will take at least ten days before you will look normal again, provided you wear a thick layer of make-up.

Different kinds of lasers

• **The CO2:** the most powerful and most frequently used laser. It's an effective way of removing brown liver spots caused by hyperactive melanocytes and also removes the fine vertical lines around the lips. Before the procedure you will have to: use a skin preparation with a base of a colour removing product enriched with vitamin A acid; have treatment to prevent herpes; take a test to assess your skin's capacity to heal.

• **The Erbium:** gentler and less hot than the CO2 and the skin recovers more quickly.

• **The Derma K:** combines the effects of the two previously-mentioned lasers and is used for the area around the eyes (see Tip 47).

> The after effects often last less long than those caused by laser treatment for an identical result. The procedure takes place under local anaesthetic. Afterwards, the patient alternates between applying dry-skin cream to the affected areas and spraying on spa water.

KEY FACTS

* There remains a risk of burns and loss of skin colour, especially if the practitioner is not highly skilled. Take care to make the right choice!

* You will have to wait three months to judge the final result. Meanwhile, wear a good covering of make-up.

Smooth, curvy legs, slender thighs and slim knees are youthful assets that should be preserved come what may. When a healthy lifestyle is not enough, medicine and surgery are there to help you.

keeping your legs beautiful

Prevent circulation problems

Some people inherit spider and varicose veins but many bring them on themselves. Excess weight, lack of exercise and bad eating habits are bound to affect your legs. Therefore, you need to stay slim, take exercise (walking, cycling, swimming), stop smoking, drink plenty of water and eat food rich in fibres. Also, don't forget to sleep with your feet elevated, to avoid crossing your legs and to move about often during your work-

●●● DID YOU KNOW?

> You can change the shape of your legs with the help of two surgical operations. Liposuction can reduce the size of flabby thighs and remove cellulite from behind the knees. It should not, however, be used on the inside of the thighs or on the ankles, because of the high risk of complications. After an incision has been made, the fat is turned to liquid and then sucked out.

> Lipotomy is a much gentler technique that requires no surgery. Physiological saline is injected into the fatty cells. This makes them

ing day. And don't rely on medicines that tone up the veins: their effectiveness is questionable.

How to eliminate varicose veins

Problems take the form of red or bluish spider's webs of fine veins and capillaries or swollen, twisted varicose veins. The specialist has various procedures at his/her disposal, depending on the seriousness of the problem.

• **Thermocoagulation:** used to treat spider veins and less serious varicose veins. A nickel needle linked to a high frequency current produces heat, which targets the red and blue blood vessels only without damaging the other tissues.

• **Sclerotherapy:** a saline solution containing an irritant substance is injected directly into the vein. This is combined with compression bandaging. The aim is to block the vein by causing inflammation in the wall of the vein and a small localized blood clot.

• **Copper vapour laser:** this is often used in conjunction with sclerotherapy.

• **Stripping:** this is the most radical method. It involves extracting the whole of the vein through a tiny incision under local or general anaesthetic.

swell and exposure to infrared rays makes them explode. However, it is not yet available in some countries, including the UK.

> Resculpturing, or remodelling, made-to-measure combines a body scrub with glycolic acid and electrotherapy (five weeks of treatments).

KEY FACTS

* Ginkgo biloba is good for the veins. It's available in pharmacies in the form of gel that is applied by means of gentle masage.

* In women with prominent varicosities, surgery often achieves a good result.

putting on weight?

Many women put on weight at about the age of 50. However, it's not always for the same reason, so the problem needs a personalized answer.

DID YOU KNOW?

> Saunas and steam baths do nothing for your figure: you lose liquid but still retain your fat.

> Behavioural therapies (relaxation, sophrology, the various forms of psychotherapy etc.) can be helpful.

> Modern drugs are available from the doctor for people with significant obesity problems.

Learn to eat differently

Your metabolism is not what it was. You must accept this and change your eating habits. A reduction in your daily calorie intake doesn't necessarily mean that you have to deprive yourself. It's a matter of reorganizing your meals by getting rid of 'empty calories', which only create fat and do the body no good at all, and replacing them with 'good calories'. You'll be able to do this yourself by reading some good books on the subject or you can consult a nutritionist and let him supervise your new approach to eating. Whichever option you choose, whether it's successful or not is entirely up to you. Remember that the key to success is not so much your willpower but your relationship with your body and the amount of pride you take in it.

To be avoided at all costs

Miracle diets! If you lose five kilos (11 lb) in a week, you won't be losing fat but muscle and most of the nutriments essential to your health. And you'll put the weight straight back on as soon as you stop dieting.

Appetite suppressants! Almost all of them have a base of thyroid hormones, diuretics, amphetamines and tranquillizers. It's true they make you thinner but at the expense of your muscles, whilst your fat is hardly affected. What is more, you run a serious risk of suffering from kidney and thyroid disorders, anxiety attacks, insomnia and more.

> Powdered food substitutes can help you, provided you replace one of the two main meals with a sachet and keep a careful note of your daily calorie intake. Check on the packet to see whether the product is rich in proteins and contains essential nutriments.

KEY FACTS

* It is normal to weigh more at 50 than you did at 20. You should try to accept this and remember that being excessively thin ages you just as much.

* Regular exercise will help you to control your weight.

A bulky or slack stomach spoils your whole figure. That's why so much emphasis is put on exercises specifically chosen to prevent this, particularly those that work the abdominals. However, if it's too late and the harm has already been done, surgery can help you.

getting back a flat stomach

Liposuction

If you simply have mass of fat that resists all exercise and dieting, you can reduce it with liposuction. After your pubic hair has been shaved off, the surgeon inserts cannulas through three incisions (of around 6 mm/¼ in). The scars will no longer be visible once the hair has grown back. The operation takes around 45 minutes under epidural or local anaesthetic, and you will have to spend only a few hours in hospital.

DID YOU KNOW?

> Abdominoplasty is a tiring and painful operation. The stomach is swollen and oedema (water retention) takes a month to disappear. The bruises fade away in about ten days. The area operated on often loses some sensitivity but this should improve after a few weeks.

> Accumulations of lymph fluid can be drawn off. The scar varies depending on the size of the operation and the quality of the skin. It can be touched up under local anaesthetic but not for six months.

Abdominoplasty

When the problem is not one of fat but of a very distended muscle wall (often called an 'abdominal apron'), a much bigger operation is needed. Firstly, it involves stretching the aponeurosis (the band of tissue that connects the muscles) and removing excess fat. The surgeon then removes the excess skin, draws the skin back down and replaces the navel. Drains are left in for three days and the stitches removed after twelve days. The length of the operation is around two hours under general anaesthetic and you will need to spend two days in hospital.

Some useful advice

It's best to turn up for the operation with your weight close to normal: if you need to diet, do so beforehand. After an abdominoplasty, wear a support girdle day and night for a month. Don't return to physical exercise too early (ask your surgeon for advice). Don't expose your skin to sunshine for two months.

KEY FACTS

* When you do expose the affected area to sunshine, protect your scars with sunblock.

* After an abdominoplasty, expect to be away from work for at least a fortnight and a gradual return to physical activities.

reshape your buttocks

Are little figure-hugging dresses beginning to cause problems? Do blouson jackets and jeans no longer make you look attractive? In other words, is your bottom no longer what it was? There are several ways of remedying this situation. Choose the one that suits you.

Electrostimulation for tone and firmness

This 'motionless exercise' is done at home using a device, looking like a cushion or pair of shorts, which is equipped with electrodes that send low frequency currents into the area concerned. Three 30 minute sessions per week should succeed in firming up your buttocks. The results will be much better if you

DID YOU KNOW?

> Reshaping the buttocks using liposuction requires great dexterity on the part of the surgeon if a round, natural shape is to be achieved. It's vital to use morphing before the procedure. It's only by seeing on the screen the shapes the specialist is proposing that you will be in a position to discuss the matter and come to a detailed agreement with him.

> The morphing can be referred to if the results don't come up to your expectations and will make it easier for you to obtain free alterations. There are risks, including infection.

combine this method with appropriate exercises and daily massages with anti-cellulite cream.

Reduce fat with mesotherapy

This technique consists of injecting a cocktail of vitamins, amino acids and other medications with numerous small needles into the area under treatment. The injections stimulate blood circulation in the area and remove excess fat, whilst boosting cellular activity. Mesotherapy achieves good results on buttocks and thighs but will not be very effective if your skin is too slack. Six to ten sessions will be needed.

Liposuction for the most serious cases

The technique is the same as that used for the stomach (see Tip 57). After the procedure you will have to wear a pair of support pants day and night for the first two weeks and all day for the following two weeks. Even if your buttocks are slack and flabby, you are likely to regain the firmness of your dreams. Touching up is possible but you'll need to wait six months.

KEY FACTS

* Besides fat, liposuction can also help tackle cellulite and reduce the orange peel effect on the skin but it will not lift up your buttocks nor make any stretch marks disappear.

* Up to about 5 litres ($8\frac{1}{2}$ pints) of fat can be sucked out during one session of liposuction.

the symptoms of depression

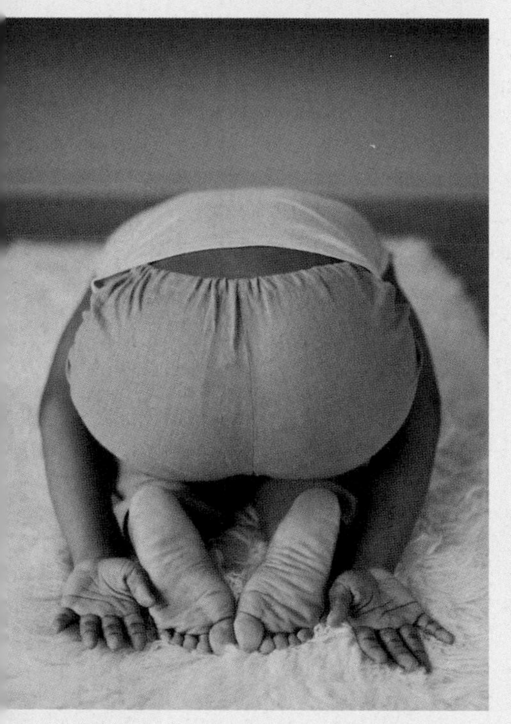

At this time of great change, you can experience times when all seems confused and futile. To help you to handle these changes and the adjustments they involve sucessfully, the help of a psychotherapist can be invaluable but take care to find the right one.

DID YOU KNOW?

> Psychotherapy developed out of psychoanalysis and has many very different branches. There are, among others, the followers of Freud and Lacan; Gestalt Therapy which emphasizes awareness of the present moment; American behavioural and cognitive therapies; Jungian therapies, which have a spiritual element.

The menopause doesn't have to mean depression

In our grandmothers' time, much was said about the melancholy caused by the mysterious and awesome 'change of life'. Today, the link between menopause and depression appears more tenuous. Of course, the reduction of oestrogens can affect morale, because it causes a shortage of serotonin (the hormone that creates a sense of well-being and euphoria). Also, the lack of sleep makes you feel less energetic during the day. However, a good hormonal replacement treatment will solve all that. If you do feel ups and downs, they are mainly caused by our society's disparaging attitude towards, or worse still, total unconcern for, women said to be 'of a certain age'. If you feel as If you have become transparent and good for nothing and, in fact, ready for the scrap heap, the analysts are there to help you.

> **Be prepared to try several of these schools to find the one that suits you best.**

Analytical psychotherapy

A psychotherapist will not prescribe tranquillizers, sleeping pills or antidepressants. His/her work relies upon verbal communication and the relationship established between you. Its aim is to help make you aware of your inner conflicts, thus enabling you to approach your life differently. What distinguishes psychotherapy from psychoanalysis is that the former takes less time and can focus on a specific problem, in this case how to deal with menopausal changes. Therapy can last several months or several years, depending on your needs – and the size of your wallet – and involves one, or several, sessions per week.

KEY FACTS

* It can take a long time to realize you are suffering from depression. Get help as soon as you are aware of the symptoms.
* Be prepared to see several therapists before making your choice. If you don't get on with one therapist, find another.

60 don't be upset by bladder problems

Some women suffer from this problem, which can be very embarrassing, from about the age of 40 onwards. Don't get all upset about it, because it can be cured.

A very urgent necessity: the more or less uncontrollable need to urinate (called an irritable bladder) is caused by overactivity of the detrusor muscle, responsible for expelling urine from the bladder. Incontinence can also be caused by weakening of the sphincter. This can have several causes: childbirth, a prolapse (when an organ moves out of its normal position), neurological illness; loss of elasticity as a result of oestrogen shortage, so fundamental to the menopause. The weakening of the sphincter can also cause wetting when coughing, sneezing or making a violent effort (known as 'stress incontinence').

Discuss your symptoms with your doctor: he/she will arrange appropriate investigations to exclude serious underlying problems. Remedies vary. Irritable bladder is treated by relaxing and antispasmodic drugs. Loss of elasticity by HRT. Prolapse of the bladder (and stress incontinence) by surgical operation.

DID YOU KNOW?

> Surgery involves the insertion of two tiny balloons made of biocompatible plastic and filled with gel. They exert pressure on the muscle and help it to stay firm.

KEY FACTS

* Incontinence caused by being 'caught short' usually affects women over 65.

* If you are younger and your urinary pattern changes radically, consult your doctor.

case study

Sharing what I know about making the second half of life great

'I'm a pharmacist and my profession has helped me understand just how important Hormonal Replacement Therapy (HRT) is for menopausal women. These little pills really change your life! I started the treatment immediately of course but I didn't stop there. I never miss an opportunity to discuss it with my female customers, to give them advice and reassurance. Some of them say they don't need it, because they don't have hot flushes. However, as I take pains to explain to them, synthetic hormones have an effect on lots of other things. We not only discuss HRT but also plant hormones and food supplements. Of course, the most important thing is talking to your doctor about it but a good chat with a pharmacist of the same age can be very useful. In fact, we all need to talk and take stock of what is happening.'

useful addresses

» Homeopathy

British Homeopathic Association
Hahnemann House
29 Park Street West
Luton LU1 3BE
tel: 0870 444 3950

The Society of Homeopaths
4a Artizan Road
Northampton NN1 4HU
tel: 01604 621400

Australian Homeopathic Association
PO Box 430, Hastings
Victoria 3915, Australia
www.homeopathyoz.org

» Herbal medicine

British Herbal Medicine Association
Sun House, Church Street
Stroud, Gloucester GL5 1JL
tel: 01453 751389

National Institute of Medical Herbalists
56 Longbrook Street
Exeter, Devon EX4 6AH
tel: 01392 426022

» Massage

British Massage Therapy Council
www.bmtc.co.uk

Association of British Massage Therapists
42 Catharine Street
Cambridge CB1 3AW
tel: 01223 240 815

European Institute of Massage
42 Moreton Street
London SW1V 2PB
tel: 020 7931 9862

» Menopause

British Menopause Society
www.the-bms.org

National Osteoporosis Society
Camerton
Bath BA2 0PJ
tel: 01761 471771
www.nos.org.uk

International Osteoporosis Foundation
www.osteofound.org

North America Menopause Society
PO Box 94527, Cleveland
Ohio 44101-4527, USA

Australasian Menopause Society
PO Box 1228, Buderim
Queensland 4556
Australia

» Relaxation therapy

British Autogenic Society
The Royal London Homoeopathic Hospital
Greenwell Street
London W1W 5BP

British Complementary Medicine Association
PO Box 5122
Bournemouth BH8 0WG
tel: 0845 345 5977

» Yoga

The British Wheel of Yoga
25 Jermyn Street
Sleaford
Lincs NG34 7RU
tel: 01529 306 851
www.bwy.org.uk

index

acknowledgements

Cover: G. George/Pix; p. 8/9: P. Boorman/Pix; p. 11: Gulliver/Zefa; p. 13: Emely/Zefa; p. 15: A. Weinbrecht/Stone; p. 20-21: M. Möllenberg/Zefa; p. 23: Emely/Zefa; p. 24-25: Miles/Zefa; p. 30-31, 35, 79: Neo Vision/Photonica; p. 37: D. Roth/Stone; p. 38: p. Leonard/Zefa; p. 41: Gulliver/Zefa; p. 43: B. Roaman/Marie Claire; p. 48-49: P. Lee Harvey/Stone; p. 51: Zefa; p. 51-52: G. & M. D. de Lossy/Image Bank; p. 55: Pinto/Zefa; p. 59: G. & M. D. de Lossy/Image Bank; p. 61: D. Rieder/Stone; p. 62: A. Nagelmann/Pix; p. 67: M. Montezin/Marie Claire; p. 69: Pinto/Zefa; p. 73: Emely/Zefa; p. 74: A. Peisl/Zefa; p. 83: G. Barto/Image Bank; p. 87: Star/Zefa; p. 89: G. George/Pix; p. 91: Peisl/Zefa; p. 92: © Akiko Ida; p. 95: G. Schuster/Zefa; p. 97: Emely/Zefa; p. 98-99: R. Daly/Stone; p. 102-103: G. & M. D. de Lossy/Image Bank; p. 105: M. Montezin/Marie Claire; p. 109: T. Anderson/Pix; p. 110: A. Parker/Option Photo; p. 113: J. Frazier/Stone; p. 114: © Akiko Ida; p. 117: M. Montezin/Marie Claire; p. 119: K. Fitzgerald/Stone; p. 121: J. Toy/Stone.

Illustrations: Hélène Lafaix pages: 4-5, 6, 16, 26-27, 64, 76 and 80.

The author would like to thank Doctor Alain Roux, gérontologue (12, quai Papacino, Nice); Marc Canavaté, Osteopath (114, Avenue du Mont-Alban, Nice); and Grand Optical stores.

• ALL THE KEYS, ALL THE TIPS TO ANSWER ALL YOUR HEALTH QUESTIONS •

60 TIPS allergies

60 TIPS anti-ageing

60 TIPS cellulite

60 TIPS detox

60 TIPS flat stomach

60 TIPS headaches

60 TIPS healthy skin

60 TIPS sleep

60 TIPS slimming

60 TIPS stress relief

Editorial director: Caroline Rolland

Editorial assistant: Alexandra Bentz

Graphic design and layout: G & C MOI

Final checking: Marie-Claire Seewald and Fabienne Hélou

Illustrations: Alexandra Bentz

Production: Felicity O'Connor

Translation: JMS Books LLP

This edition published in 2004 by Hachette Illustrated UK, Octopus Publishing Group Ltd., 2–4 Heron Quays, London E14 4JP

English translation by JMS Books LLP (email: moseleystrachan@blueyonder.co.uk)

A CIP catalogue for this book is available from the British Library

ISBN: 1 84430 073 0

Printed in Singapore by Tien Wah Press